Praise

'Charmaine has been my nutritionist for the last few years and recently my children's too. I have benefited from the amazing home remedies which she provides. My immunity to common coughs and colds has increased due to her nut mixtures. Her over all approach to being healthy has become so fluid with my family's daily life. I would like to thank her as we have enhanced our life from all her experience and dedication to the field of health'—**Ami Modi, Firestone Diamonds**

'As a fitness enthusiast, I strive to maintain my energy levels. Charmaine has helped me do so. Her book will be a ready reckoner for all those looking to stay fit and healthy'—**Anita Dongre, Fashion Designer**

'Charmaine's powder remedies are magical as they cure and improve any specific ailments which need to be addressed, while also working on the individual's general well being'—**Apoorva Mehta, CEO, Dharma Productions**

'It has been my privilege to have known and worked with Charmaine for seven years. Her nutrition plans helped me restore my hormonal balance without the use of any allopathic medication, and helped me maintain good health through and after my pregnancy. What I enjoy most about working with Charmaine is that she makes use of everyday kitchen ingredients as dietary supplements and works with your dietary preferences to improve your overall health and well being'—**Ashika Pohoomul Mehta, MSW**

'Charmaine's naturopathy therapy helped me stay fit and glowing all through my pregnancy'—**Ekta Raheja, K. Reheja Universal**

'In today's age of artificial flavours and sweeteners, Charmaine's homemade remedies have proven to be organic, simple and extremely result oriented. Natural is the way to go!'—**Siddharth Malhotra, Actor**

'Charmaine did her internship under me when I was Chief Dietician at SL Raheja Hospital. I was able to gauge her commitment and dedication way back in 1990 and she imbibed good practices of nutrition. I am proud that she has worked hard to reach where she has today. She justifies my considering her as my star pupil'—**Gourpriya D. Koppikar R.D., Consultant Dietician, Bombay Hospital**

'Charmaine's programme worked like magic for me. I met her on November 30, 2007, and by October 2008, I had lost 19 kg! Isn't that magic?'—**Hiroo Yash Johar, Producer, Dharma Productions**

'I started using Charmaine's remedies eighteen months ago, and mentally and physically, I have never felt better. She has a very natural approach to things and it is refreshing and comforting. With my cholesterol levels under control now, I am focusing on monitoring other problem areas. It's been a life changing experience'—**Kajal Assomull, Jewellery Designer**

'I have been following Charmaine's advice for a couple of years now in order to maintain my energy, fitness, and thyroid levels. As an actor and politician I need to be at my healthiest and Charmaine's spice mixes ensure that I continue to be blessed with good health!'—**Kirron Kher, Actor and Politician**

'Charmaine is not just a nutritionist of exceptional ability, she's a magician. She has a complete understanding of the human body and her diet is individually crafted to suit your medical condition and history. Consequently, her prescribed regimen gets results beyond ones expectations'—**Madhu and Mohammed Khan, Founder Enterprise Nexus**

'My passion, which happens to be fashion, has governed my life to the exclusion of everything else, for over a decade. Suddenly, one day, I actually saw myself in the mirror and could not recognize my own reflection! Physical beauty, as much as clothes, holds tremendous importance to me and my own appearance was belying this very fact. It was imperative for me to get back into shape and that too, super fast! Having heard really good things about Charmaine's work in the field of nutrition and naturopathy, I decided to get in touch with her. Believe me, it's been an incredible journey toward a fitter me'—**Manav Gangwani, Couturier Delhi**

'I started Charmaine's programme soon after I had my baby and wanted to shed the excess baby weight in a natural and healthy way. She not only helped me do this by giving me powder recepies made from ingredients in my kitchen but also gradually transformed my health in totality by giving me homemade remedies to cure common ailments for me and my son, which built our immunity in general making my approach more naturopathic'—**Natasha Poonawalla, Poonawalla Group**

'Charmaine has helped both of us regulate and create balance in our systems with her natural approach and remedy. We feel our ailments have come under control under her guidance and supervision'—**Nayana and Shailendra Singh, JMD Percept**

'Charmaine can cure ailments which medication can't! It could be diabetes, thyroid, obesity, or PCOD. Whenever my family or I face any health issue, we call Charmaine. I have total faith in her. We are all addicted to Charmaine and her powders!'—**Neetu Singh Kapoor, Actor**

'Charmaine is the queen of nutrition. She knows it all. She has helped me lose a lot of weight and keep a balance of all my blood levels'—**Nitasha Nanda, Escorts Group Delhi**

'Charmaine helped me lose all my pregnancy weight and achieve my target!'—**Riddhima Kapoor Sahni, Designer**

'I have been on Charmaine's powders for over six months now and I am pleased to say that she has made me feel healthier, more energetic and glowing!'—**Roopa Fabiani, Fabiani Group**

'My mundane kitchen ingredients turn into miracle cures with Charmaine's magic!'—**Sarita Garware Ramsay, JMD Garware Group**

'Charmaine is my 911 any time I'm sick, even before I call my doctor. And she always comes to my rescue. I run all my medical prescription by her and she has a natural solution to everything! I've been with her for years now. She has helped me through so many health issues, taught me to eat right and think healthy! And the best part is that she is so accessible—always responsive, no matter where she is. I carry her powders and water infusions all over the world, and they have worked wonders for me'—**Suman Manghnani, Hotelier**

'Charmaine has been a blessing—keeping us healthy with natural inputs and away from tabs and pills. Her friendly and accessible nature makes the relationship fun and productive. Charmaine is now a friend, necessity ... addiction'—**Sumi and Jaspal Bindra, Group ED and CEO, Standard Chartered HK**

'Charmaine has helped me and my family maintain good health over the past few years. Her simple and practical diet plans, therapeutic waters, and spice mixes have helped ensure good blood reports and overall fitness despite our hectic lifestyles and travel schedules'—**Swapnali Bhosale Kadam, ABIL Group**

'Charmaine is my godsent angel who with her vast knowledge of naturopathy has healed me and my family. I needed to heal quickly post my operation and wanted to get there naturally. Charmaine guided me through this with her expertise, patience, love, and care. I am forever grateful to her. She continues to look after me and my family in our daily stress-filled lives, building our immunity and helping in our mental and physical well being'—**Vaibhavi Merchant, Bollywood Choreographer**

'Meeting Charmaine changed my concept of long term medication altogether. By sheer coincidence I discovered I had thyroid disorder. Her fascinating yet purely SPICY medication was just the most amazing. I have ever experienced. I followed it like the bible and now I am as good as new (which my endocrinologist said would be lifelong and so would the medication). Thank you Charmaine!'—**Zahra Morani, Cineyug Production**

'Charmaine's plan for good health is like magic. I was amazed when I first met her and was given a plan of natural herbs and spices to cure me of my hormonal imbalance. Within six months I was cured without having to put chemicals into my body. Charmaine's natural spices, that I put together in my own kitchen, was like a magic potion…really a big blessing in my life. I no longer need to deal with side effects of dangerous tablets because I have cured myself the natural way. I intend on following her plans for the rest of my life so I look and feel healthy inside out!'—**Zoa Morani, Actress and Producer**

kitchen clinic
good health always with Charmaine

Charmaine D'Souza

EBURY
PRESS

An imprint of Penguin Random House

EBURY PRESS

USA | Canada | UK | Ireland | Australia
New Zealand | India | South Africa | China | Singapore

Ebury Press is part of the Penguin Random House group of companies
whose addresses can be found at global.penguinrandomhouse.com

Published by Penguin Random House India Pvt. Ltd
4th Floor, Capital Tower 1, MG Road,
Gurugram 122 002, Haryana, India

First published by Random House India 2013

Copyright © Charmaine D'Souza 2013

Illustration copyright © Madhurya Balan 2013

All rights reserved

10 9 8 7 6 5 4 3 2

ISBN 9788184003192

Typeset in Adobe Garamond by R. Ajith Kumar
Printed at Repro India Limited

This book is sold subject to the condition that it shall not, by way of trade
or otherwise, be lent, resold, hired out, or otherwise circulated without the
publisher's prior consent in any form of binding or cover other than that in
which it is published and without a similar condition including this condition
being imposed on the subsequent purchaser.

www.penguin.co.in

This is a legitimate digitally printed version of the book and therefore might not
have certain extra finishing on the cover.

To my husband Savio and my daughters
Charlyene and Savlyene

Contents

PART 3: USING HERBS TO PREVENT AND CURE MAJOR ILLNESSES

PART 4: GROW YOUR OWN KITCHEN GARDEN

Foreword

I AM AN AVID READER WHO LIKES TO KEEP ABREAST OF HEALTH and dietary issues; I'm also a constant worrier about food and its nutrients. So my curiosity was piqued when I first heard about Charmaine's work. After meeting her, I began to understand the nature of foods. There are foods that are good for you and there are foods that aren't. Understanding how food works solves most of our dietary issues and keeps us in the best of health. For me, Charmaine represents the world of naturopathy and healthy eating. It is with her that I first started my good eating habits.

My father was always a fit and exuberant man but a sudden heart attack took away much of his zest and energy. His failing health transformed me from an ice-cream-loving child to a health-conscious eater. Having had an ailing father at home who was suffering from different ailments for quite some time, it was fascinating for me to understand the cause of my father's ill health. Charmaine came into my life many years after that incident. In retrospect, I wish our paths had crossed earlier because she has given me clarity about food and its many intricacies.

Though I am an actor, and actors are often scrutinized about how they look, I'm also a foodie, so it's very important for me to have met someone like Charmaine who doesn't restrict me from eating but instead gives me guidelines as to how I can balance my diet. All these years I have never been on a low-cal or restricted diet and I never want to be on one because that goes against my inherent foodie nature! Charmaine's programme and simple plans make me feel extremely healthy and charged.

My advice to my fellow readers is to do what is best for your body. Understand what works for you and also how food works. One should be a little aware of the food they eat today, with so much adulteration going around.

> Stick to home food at least 320 days of the year and you will stay fit and healthy.

This book will be beneficial to those you want to be healthy every day of their lives. Be an intelligent eater. The rewards are infinite.

Rani Mukerji

Introduction

MY STORY

AS A 5-YEAR-OLD, I REMEMBER MY MOTHER TAKING US TO THE pool every day for a swim. A nutritious snack would always be packed and taken along so that we wouldn't pester her to buy us those batata wadas available right outside the pool complex. So, nearly forty years ago, while other kids would rush from the pool to Simla Canteen for their daily fix of deep-fried snacks, we would be fed sprouted moong, boiled egg chappati wraps, fruit, and dahi. We envied the other kids but my mother would always tell us that all the calories they had burned swimming would soon be piled on with the very first bite!

When I was a year old, my father developed diabetes. I spent most of my childhood watching him try to keep his blood sugars under control. A friend of his introduced him to an ayurvedic practitioner who would give him packets filled with ayurvedic powders. They were so bitter tasting that he would have to fill them in gel capsules and then swallow them. So every Saturday, we kids would sit around the dining table and help him fill empty capsules with the medicine. Our eyes would water and we would constantly be sneezing. I can still vividly recollect the scene. Unfortunately, this form of treatment never helped him decrease his blood sugars. There was also a doubt regarding the lead and other heavy metal content of the powders. Ultimately, he succumbed to cancer of the gall bladder and spleen.

When I started my career in the field of nutrition and dietetics, I knew I wanted to help people by first educating them about their disease and giving them informed choices. After studying naturopathy I was further able to help patients use kitchen ingredients to make their own therapeutic powder and water. Since I gave out the recipe for the powders to be made by them in their own kitchens, I knew that there would never be any doubt about adulteration/allopathic drugs being slyly introduced into the powders. Even today when my patients/clients consume their powders at a party or a dinner and they are warned about taking any suspicious sort of treatment, they confidently inform their friends that the only place where adulterants can be added is in their own kitchen and their kitchen help would never do anything to hamper their treatment.

My first internship was in 1990 at KEM Hospital, Mumbai. I was lucky to have been offered a double internship…so while the rest of my batch mates were enjoying their vacation I started my second internship at the SL Raheja Hospital, Mumbai, under Dr Koppikar, who still is my inspiration, mentor, and guide. She offered me my first job as a locum at the hospital but a year later I knew I wanted to do something different from what the others in my field were doing. So I started lecturing on food and nutrition at Jaslok Hospital and a number of catering colleges. For eighteen years I taught the subject and also continued my private practice. However, in 2008, I set up a full-time practice. Today, here I am…perusing blood reports, empathizing with people who are unwell, taking dietary recalls, using my monitors to check them, listing out ingredients for their powders and waters…doing this all on a one-on-one basis and enjoying every minute of it.

I can very proudly say that my 23-year-old practice is solely based on word of mouth referrals. I would like to think of all my clients as superstars in their own way, but Vinod Khanna was the first Bollywood film star I wrote out a diet plan for. I had already met many of Mumbai's top industrialists before that but Mr Khanna bowled me over when he served me water and also took the tray back into the kitchen!

I start each day with the recitation of the Rosary and I also say a prayer before prescribing/jotting down a therapeutic powder. I am humbled by the faith people have in me; it overwhelms me and sometimes even scares me. They are so sure I will be able to help them, even though there are times when I am in doubt. There are times when they call to let me know what their specialist has advised them and want to know if he/she is on the right track and that is when I have to remind them that I am only their nutritionist naturopath…not their doctor. This implicit faith my clients have in me makes me do what I do daily.

My 'Good Health Always' Programme

I am often asked about the 'holistic' approach that I prescribe. A holistic approach considers the whole person and how he/she interacts with his/her environment. They are motivated by how good they feel when they find reserves of energy and enthusiasm for life, and by the knowledge that their health is truly in their hands.

My **Good Health Always** programme is holistic and follows a natural, therapeutic approach towards achieving good health through self-cleansing. **The main objective of the programme is the prevention of illness or the cure of ailments, with the use of kitchen herbs and spices so that the body maintains and heals itself.** Naturopathic programmes treat people, not merely the symptoms of a disease, by removing the cause of the ailment. The fact that the recipe of the mix is always given to the client ensures that the individual can take an active part in maintaining good health…always!

The mix is tailor-made to suit a client's specific set of ailments and takes into consideration his or her dietary intake, medical supplementation, lifestyle, and activity. The fact that the ingredients for the mix are often found within the reach of your own kitchen or at your nearest grocery shop adds to the ease in making it in your own home.

My clients keep coming back to me because they see results! The lady who was my first private patient still takes my advice for her great grandson! And likewise, I do hope that this book enriches the lives of all my readers.

DIETETICS

My work involves the blend of two very important fields: naturopathy and dietetics. So to understand what I do, it is first necessary to understand what these fields are. They both require follow-ups and working closely with the patients. I'll start by telling you about the main role of a dietitian.

Dietetics focuses on the interaction between nutrition and health. Dietitians and dietetic technicians design something called 'nutrition therapies' that help the body use the natural nutrients and properties in food to protect against disease and promote health. A dietitian is an expert in food and nutrition. He/she gives dietary advice, helps promote healthy eating habits, and also helps in developing specific diets for people. Dietitians translate the science of nutrition into everyday information about food for health and well being, and use this information to treat patients.

The day-to-day work of a dietitian often includes:

❖ educating clients on how food and healthy eating habits, help prevent illness, and achieve and maintain optimum health;

❖ educating and advising a wide range of patients about the advantages of therapeutic diets and dietary therapy and how they manage their conditions;

❖ calculating the patient's nutritional requirements using usual tests based on evaluations of blood chemistry, temperature, stress, mobility, and other significant factors;

❖ analyzing the nutritional content of the food a patient regularly intakes;

❖ devising eating plans and changing recipes for better nutrition;
❖ educating additional healthcare and non-healthcare professionals about food and nutrition issues;
❖ working with corporations to support well being programmes for their employees, as well as advising catering departments about precise dietary requirements;
❖ writing reports and case notes and maintaining correct records;
❖ carrying out appointments in people's homes, including nursing homes; and
❖ counselling the food and pharmaceutical industries.

Now, onto naturopathy.

NATUROPATHY

Naturopathy developed out of the ancient healing customs of Europe, with its roots resolutely grounded in early Greek medical philosophy. Naturopathy is now increasingly being acknowledged by mainstream medicine as a valuable and efficient system for treating a range of disorders.

Naturopathy often uses dietetics to treat patients, however dietetics in itself is a very focused field. I combine the two, to the best of my abilities, so that I can help the patient in the best possible way.

My method

I use an investigational process known as EQ4 meridien testing. The EQ4 equipment accesses the energy flow via the meridian channels in the fingers and the palms of both hands. The EQ4 introduces an imperceptible electric current to measure the resistance of the acupressure points. About 50 points are tested and an overall snapshot of the organ system is obtained. Based on all this information, I formulate a programme tailor-made for the client from a vast database of healing remedies that will ultimately bring the unbalanced points and meridians into a state of balance.

Each and every one of us has to be a master of our mind and body and hence of our destiny. We need to understand how our body functions and this is an important step in our approach toward physical and mental wellness. Our body has the ability to heal itself if only we can learn to listen to it and respond by giving it what it really needs. In spite of all the years of abuse our body endures through exposure to environmental pollutants and toxins, poor nutrition, smoking and alcohol consumption, inactivity and emotional upheavals, it usually serves us well for many years before starting to break down and show signs of ill health.

If you intend to begin on a new route to good health and well being, I would strongly advise that you first undergo a thorough medical examination. Ensure that along with your routine blood tests you also test your glycosylated hemoglobin levels and apolipoproteins. Then sit down and **draw up a list of all your ailments, your dietary recall, your health history, as well as a family history of major health issues like cancer and diabetes**. Also put down a list of all the medicines and supplements you take on a daily basis. All this information will enable your healthcare practitioner to easily assess your health status and help you get back on the road to recovery as quickly as possible.

Stay blessed with good health...always!

Charmaine D'Souza
June, Mumbai

PART 1

UNDERSTANDING HERBS

1

What is Naturopathy?

WHY NATUROPATHY?

BELIEVERS IN NATUROPATHY ARE OFTEN VERY FEW, AND IN today's technologically advanced world, we are skeptical about ancient practices.

Radhika, a patient of mine, is the epitome of a modern woman. By the time she was 28, she was happily married and had two children. One day, she stopped getting her period. This continued for six months, after which she spoke to her friend, who was a gynaecologist. To Radhika's surprise, she found out that it was the early onset of menopause.

Convinced that it was a good thing, since she wasn't planning on having more children, she went out with her mother (who was 54 years old, and going through menopause at that point of time) for lunch. After hearing her mother talk about menopause and its troubling aspects, she realized that she was going through the same thing as her mother, twenty-four years earlier she should! Radhika, of course, got really worried at the fact that she was ageing early and asked her mother for advice. Her mother, who happened to be a patient of mine, got her to meet me. And so her treatment began.

Radhika got her period after two months of my treatment. And again. She also conceived and aborted twice in a span of six months. Radhika is now a strong believer in the powers of naturopathy. She is 35 years old now, and she still gets her periods regularly.

Even if you don't believe, like Radhika, in naturopathy, there must have been those countless times when you've found yourself tired and exhausted with no clue as to why or what you can do to snap out of the funk and re-energize yourself. Happens, doesn't it? Now if you had a quick cure to kill that headache, which required you to just rummage in your kitchen, wouldn't it be brilliant? Something that is easy to make, and not too difficult to inculcate in the hectic lives that we lead today? Just a little bit of this and a little bit of that and voila...cured! This, to a certain extent, is the root of naturopathy.

Naturopathy has been prevalent in India since the Vedic times. Its various forms have been practised in India for centuries, and it's only recently that allopathy has caught up. Many of the foundations of naturopathy—such as the importance of diet, clean fresh water, sunlight, exercise, and stress management—have been adopted by conventional medicine too.

The lives we live today are so full of pressures and deadlines; the food we eat is not nourishing enough and sleep is a distant memory. Adding a lot of medicines to this lifestyle for things that we can cure with a few simple remedies seems unnecessary, don't you think? In this book, I'll talk about those few simple remedies that you can make yourself.

Let's begin with a little introduction to naturopathy.

NATUROPATHY IS GUIDED BY SIX FOUNDATIONAL PRINCIPLES

❖ The healing power of nature
❖ First do no harm
❖ Find and treat the cause, not only the symptom
❖ Always treat the whole person, not only their disease
❖ Education
❖ Prevention

Naturopathy believes that the body is capable of healing itself in the proper circumstances and conditions. For example, if the pH of blood is maintained as near to neutral as possible then a lot of diseases can be avoided.

Naturopathy uses various treatments, which stimulate the healing powers that are present in the body itself. Nutritional medicine, dietetics, herbal medicine, homeopathy, lifestyle changes, and treatments like massage, acupressure, or alternative healing treatments like the Bowen technique (named after the Australian industrial chemist Tom Bowen) are usually the different kind of treatments involved in naturopathy. The Bowen technique includes 30- to 45-minute sessions in which there are gentle rolling motions along the muscles and tendons with 2-minute pauses between each muscle group. The pauses are to allow the body to 'reset' itself.

NATUROPATHY AIMS TO

❖ Minimize symptoms
❖ Support the body's vital force (its capacity to self-heal)
❖ Re-balance the system so that illness is less likely to occur in the future
❖ Educate the patients to look after their own health and the health of their family

Commonly treated disorders using naturopathy include:
❖ fatigue
❖ digestive complaints
❖ mood disorders and depression
❖ allergies and sensitivities
❖ behavioural problems
❖ chronic fatigue syndrome
❖ musculoskeletal complaints such as arthritis
❖ cardiovascular (heart and blood vessel) problems
❖ high blood pressure
❖ fertility problems
❖ endocrine disturbances
❖ hormonal imbalances, such as premenstrual tension and menopause

ASSESSMENT BY A NATUROPATH

A naturopath doesn't just treat the illness; he/she treats the cause of it. For this purpose, a naturopath needs to know about your diet, lifestyle, family background, and environment as well as the history behind your illness and/or problem. As well as taking a detailed health history, the naturopath may use other diagnostic techniques, such as:

❖ iris analysis
❖ kinesiology
❖ blood analysis
❖ stool and urine analysis
❖ hair analysis
❖ functional testing

TREATMENT BY A NATUROPATH

Treatment involves a lot of things, and a naturopath has to be aware of your daily lifestyle, amount of stress, and, of course, your eating habits to actually start treatment. An important thing that a naturopath always ensures is to make the treatment as comfortable for you as possible. A naturopath employs a range of non-invasive techniques and these include (but are not limited to):

❖ **Nutrition and dietary advice**: being one of the founding principles of naturopathy, it is imperative to eat whole, fresh, unprocessed foods. A poor diet is harmful as it stops the body from functioning well and the toxins can cause various diseases.

❖ **Herbal medicine**: is useful as Western medicine and can be used to extremely effectively.

❖ **Homeopathy**: is used to stimulate the immune system.

❖ **Hydrotherapy (water therapy)**: involves the use of hot and cold compresses for certain conditions to influence the flow of blood and body heat in our bodies.

❖ **Physical therapies**: in naturopathy generally include massages, Bowen technique, acupressure, bio-puncture, etc.

❖ **Counselling techniques**: emotional problems and stress can interfere with the healing process. Counseling, combined with naturopathy, can help resolve these issues.

Naturopathy is a very important aspect of my work, and it helps you, as a reader, to understand me too. As you now know, herbs and spices form the root of what I do. Let's go on to learn about the main herbs and spices and discover the mojo that lies in them!

2

The Medicinal Power of Herbs, Spices, and Other Ingredients

HERBS HAVE POWERS. THEY ARE INDEED MAGICAL THINGS. NO, not just to make your food taste brilliant but also in your lives, and more specifically, in naturopathy treatments.

Did you know, for instance, that drinking water with star anise is a good way to energize your system? It is equivalent to a caffeine shot. I normally recommend that water infused with star anise should be consumed only till 7 pm. Otherwise, trust me, you won't sleep till 2 am!

Here is a list of different herbs and their properties. *A note of warning: consult your naturopath before taking them or combining them yourself.*

Acai Berry

Acai, the celebrity berry, made popular by Oprah Winfrey on her talk show. The acai berry is fantastic because of its incredibly high levels of antioxidants. It is also rich in proteins, fibre, Vitamin E, minerals, and essential Omega oils—its fatty acid ratio is similar to that of olive oil, and is thought to be a contributing factor to low incidence of heart diseases in Mediterranean countries. **The fruit's protein content is more than what is found in an average egg.**

The acai berry is an energy enhancer, aphrodisiac, and weight-loss aid. It has the ability to boost energy and stamina, slow down the effects of ageing, and prevent the development of certain cancers. Its high antioxidant content has shown to slow down the effects of ageing.

These wonder berries also prevent heart attacks, protect the spread of bacterial infections, mitigating the effects of diabetes, easing inflammation, and thwarting the development of neurological diseases. This is also a major superfood (discussed later in the chapter). **People have been using acai berry to get that age-defying beauty, energy, improved vision, stronger heart, and better mental clarity.** They are also a natural cholesterol controller.

AGAVE SYRUP

The discerning eater prefers to use agave syrup as it is made up of fructose rather than glucose, which makes it easier to absorb (which means the body uses less insulin to break it down). It doesn't significantly raise blood sugar levels because of its very low glycemic index (GI), making it highly suitable for people with sugar sensitivities.

Agave syrup makes a good alternative to honey, maple syrup, dates, sugar, and other sweeteners.

ALLSPICE

Allspice? Isn't it a weird name to have? The British gave the tree its name because they couldn't decide which spice it was! Allspice has notes of cinnamon, nutmeg, and cloves. **It has been traditionally used as a digestion stimulant to cure flatulence.** It is also used to treat rheumatism and arthritis as it is anti-inflammatory and soothes the joints and muscles. Allspice is also used to treat stomach aches, vomiting, diarrhoea, and fever. Women can also use it to soothe menstrual cramps. It is also used to treat diabetes.

ALMONDS (BADAM)

In India, a common retort to when you forget something is—'Badam khao! ('Eat almonds!'). **Almonds are given as 'brain food' to children in India.** It is a wonder drug in itself; it lowers the risk of gall stones and lowers high blood pressure, and also helps control cardiovascular disease and diabetes. They reduce the blood sugar level, weight and LDL (bad) cholesterol. They are known to keep the heart and blood healthy. Also, almonds improve the skin. The ancient Romans actually showered newly-weds with almonds as a fertility charm!

ANISEED (SAUNF KE BEEJ)

Aniseed can relieve flatulence and phlegm from the bronchial tube. Tea made from aniseed is helpful in digestion in adults. The essential oils that give it these properties also induces a lot of perspiration and urination, thereby cleansing the body. **It also acts as a first aid solution—it can also be given to someone having convulsions.**

APRICOTS (JARDALU)

In English folklore, dreaming of apricots is said to be good luck. Apricots are brilliant laxatives and are immensely effective in the treatment of constipation.

They aid in digestion if consumed before a meal. It is an excellent food remedy for anaemia because of its high iron content. Fresh juice of apricot leaves is useful in treating skin diseases. Skin damage due to scabies, eczema, sunburns, itching of skin due to cold exposure, etc., can be reversed if apricots are applied regularly.

ASAFOETIDA (HING)

Asafoetida is traditionally used as a carminative (to prevent the formation of gas) and effectively cures various digestive disorders like colic and stomach spasms, acidity, intestinal worms, and digestive weakness. **Minute quantities of asafoetida in food are beneficial for proper digestion.** The strong, unpleasant smell of hing has earned it the uncomplimentary names 'Stinking Gum' and 'Devil's Dung'!

It has been used in treating mood swings and depression too. The pungent odour of asafoetida is supposed to calm hysteria and epilepsy. Conventional medicines use asafoetida in healing painful menstrual cramps. **It is known to be an opium antidote, and administered on opium addicts.**

BAY LEAF (TEJ PATTA)

The aromatic bay leaf, an indispensable ingredient in Indian cooking, has been proved to be highly effective in treating migraines, diabetes, and gastric ulcers. It is quite beneficial in cases of bacterial and fungal infections. Bay leaves are frequently used in aromatherapy due to their aromatic properties. They are also used in the treatment of rheumatism, amenorrhea, and colic. They also maintain the sugar level in the blood level, pulse rate, and blood pressure. They improve the immune system of the body and thus act as an anti-viral agent.

Bay leaf is also used as an antidote to poison. The fruits are extremely useful in case of abnormal vaginal discharge.

BETEL LEAF (MAGHAI PAAN)

The betel leaf is used as a wrap for all the spices and sugar candy and gulkand that is put into the paan. An effective anti-wormal agent and anti-infection agent, it also helps in normalizing the digestive tract in the case of an infection. **It provides strength to the cardiovascular system and also helps cure constipation.**

BISHOP'S WEED (AJWAIN)

Ajwain stimulates the appetite and enhances digestion. It has anti-acidic properties. It is used as an antiseptic and for cleaning wounds and treating skin infections. Ajwain seeds are also used in prevention of bad breath. Ajwain is furthermore used to treat cholera and diarrhoea.

Aroma from crushed ajwain seeds provides respite in heavy colds and migraine headaches. Its oil is used in eardrops for ear aches. Ajwain has anti-spasmodic properties and the seeds are said to relax the uterus and provide relief from menstrual cramps. This herb contains several chemicals, including those which are used to make prescription medications!

BLACK SESAME SEEDS (KAALA TILL)

The famous saying 'open sesame' (Ali Baba anyone?) came from the sesame seed pod, which bursts open when ripe. Black sesame seeds are generally very good in improving the health of bowels, hence promoting the health of the kidneys, liver, and regulating bowel movements. The seeds replenish essential body minerals, helping patients recover from serious illness and fevers much faster. They also help prevent illness by reducing cholesterol levels.

BLUEBERRIES

Blueberries have antioxidants and helps in anti-ageing. They may reduce the build-up of bad cholesterol that contributes to cardiovascular disease and stroke. They also help in the prevention of urinary tract infections. Blueberries help ease eye fatigue.

If consumed on a regular basis, blueberries greatly reduce blood sugar levels and prevent replication of the Hepatitis C virus.

Here's a baking tip: if dusted with flour right before adding them to the batter, blueberries do not sink!

Caraway Seeds (Kaala jeera)

Caraway is used for digestive problems such as heartburn, bloating, flatulence, loss of appetite, and mild spasms of the stomach and intestines. Oil from caraway seeds is also useful in improving bladder control, killing bacteria in the body, coughing up phlegm, and relieving constipation in patients. **Women use caraway oil to induce menstruation in case of delays and relieve menstrual cramps; nursing mothers use it to increase the flow of breast milk.**

Cardamom (Elaichi)

Our ancestors around the world, the Romans, Arabs, and the Chinese, have been using cardamom in their medicinal healing for ages. **Green cardamom** is great in treating dental conditions such as infections in the teeth, gums, and even the throat. It also relieves congestion of the lungs preventing pulmonary tuberculosis, inflammation of eyelids and also helping digestive disorders. **It has even been reported to be used as an antidote for scorpion and snake bites.**

Black cardamom relieves formation of gases in the stomach. It has a pleasant and soothing impact on the mucus membranes. **It is widely used to treat abnormal increase in appetite.** This plant also plays a very important part in the treatments of health issues like ulcers and inflammations. Black cardamom is a mild aphrodisiac and is used to treat a variety of male health issues. **Prolonged usage of black cardamom has been proved to improve vision.**

Cashew (Kaaju)

Cashews are antiseptic, anti-dysenteric, antibacterial, anti-ulcerous, as well as an astringent. **It is mainly used to cure diarrhoea, dysentery, and colic as an internal and external antiseptic against bacterial infections.** In addition, cashews are also used for stomach ulcers and for ear and eye infections to stop bleeding and heal wounds. Interestingly, cashews belong to the same family as pistachios, mangoes, and poison ivy!

Celery (Ajmud)

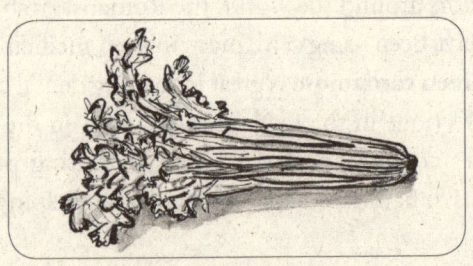

Celery is used to treat joint pain, gout, hysteria, nervousness, headache, weight loss due to malnutrition, loss of appetite, and exhaustion. It is also used to help relax and sleep, and to destroy bacteria in the urinary tract. It is used as a digestive aid and to control bowel movements, start menstruation, manage flatulence, increase sexual desire, decrease the flow of breast milk, stimulate glands, treat menstrual discomfort, and last but not the least, purify blood.

CHIA SEEDS

Chia seeds are believed to have been used by Aztec warriors and runners, allowing them to sustain themselves over an entire day just on a tablespoon of the seeds. It was the third most important crop for the Aztecs, who recognized it as a 'superfood' and prized it so highly that it was often used as currency. Chia helps to build endurance, as well as muscles and tissues.

Chia forms a barrier between carbohydrates and enzymes, thereby slowing down production of sugar, which obviously helps diabetes patients tremendously.

CHIVES

As per gypsy folklore, hanging dried bunches of chives in the house drive away disease and evil influences! Chives stimulate the appetite and promote good digestion. It can be used to ease an upset stomach, reduce flatulence, clear the nasal passage, and also prevent bad breath. When combined with a low salt diet they substantially reduce high blood pressure. They also have a mild diuretic effect. Furthermore, it shows anti-tumour effects due to its high flavonol content. When included as a part of regular diet, Chives helps in lowering high cholesterol levels in blood.

CINNAMON (DALCHINI/TAAJ)

Ever wondered why most high-calorie foods—such as French toast, cinnamon buns and all the delicious lattes—have cinnamon as toppings? **This is because cinnamon is an excellent fat burner**. It is more effective as a local stimulant rather than a general one. It is generally taken in powdered form or as on infusion when added with other medicines. It stops vomiting, relieves flatulence, and when added with steamed rice it helps to control diarrhoea and haemorrhage of the womb. *Psst.* It is also the magic ingredient for an excellent apple pie.

CLOVES (LAUNG)

Cloves are a magic spice. They have many properties that cure and repel. For instance, the smell of cloves repels flies and clove oil can kill those pesky ants that find their way into the house during the Monsoon. **Cloves have powerful germicidal properties and are used extensively in dental care for relieving toothache, sore gums, and oral ulcers.** An effective aid for food poisoning, clove oil effectively kills many forms of bacterial infections from contaminated foods. It is antiseptic and antifungal and is an excellent aid for skin disorders such as acne.

Clove oil relaxes the mind, reduces mental exhaustion and fatigue. Depression, anxiety, memory loss and insomnia have also known to have been improved by regular use of clove oil.

Not only do cloves purify the blood, it also helps in stabilizing blood sugar levels. The antiviral and cleansing properties of cloves purify the body, augmenting our resistance to disease.

Cloves are powerful combatants against gas and bloating. They also relieve the discomfort of peptic ulcers, and are effective for stomach-related conditions including nausea, hiccups, motion sickness, and vomiting.

CORIANDER (DHANIYA)

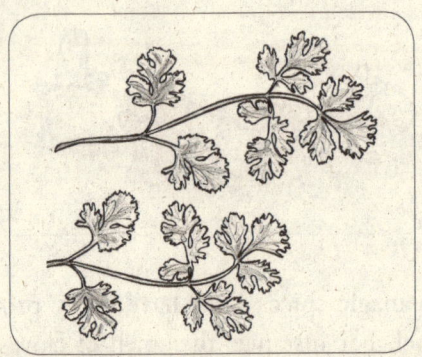

Green chutneys and garnishes in Indian food have to have flavourful dhaniya. **Coriander has three main uses: it's a good treatment for digestive ills, nervousness, and diseases of an infectious nature.**

In conventional medicine, it has been used to decrease gas, manage bowel movements, ease nervousness, reduce fevers and increase the appetite as well. The coriander seed and leaf are extremely helpful in treating dysentery, flu, vomiting, chicken pox, glandular enlargement, measles, hernia, insomnia, haemorrhoids, nausea, thirst, cold and coughs, piles, stomach ache, swellings, anxiety and gastritis. Phew. That's quite a long list!

CRANBERRY

Remember all those times when you've been told to have coconut water when you have a bout of urinary tract infection?

Well, you can have cranberry juice instead. **Cranberry fruits are used for a variety of problems, such as wounds, urinary disorders, diarrhoea, diabetes, stomach ailments, and liver problems.**

Moreover, cranberry has also been accounted to have antioxidant and anti-cancer properties.

CUMIN (JEERA)

A dish of yellow daal without the jeera ka tadka is incomplete in both taste and flavour. Cumin reduces superficial inflammation and pain. Apart from kindling the appetite, it digests food and reduces pain experienced during indigestion, flatulence, or heaviness of stomach. It also purifies blood.

Cumin seeds reduce inflammation of the uterus and increases milk production in lactating mothers. **Cumin is a skin-friendly herb and helps reduces itching.**

CURRY LEAVES (KADIPATTA)

Most of us have definitely picked out these leaves from our sambhar or upma and done away with them, blissfully ignorant of the rich iron content that they have. Curry leaves have plenty of Vitamin A and calcium. They also contain good amounts of amino acids. The leaves tend to excite the taste buds. Ulcers caused due to excessive acid secretion in the stomach, diarrhoea, and other such problems can be reversed by the use of curry leaves. It also prevents deposition of fat in various parts of the body. **Curry leaves are known to be effective in treating premature greying.**

DATES (KHAJUR)

Dates are easily digestible. They supply instant energy. Dates are considered to be an excellent cure for intestinal and digestive disorders. They effectively check the growth of pathological organisms and help in the growth of probiotic bacteria in the intestines, and can be used as a good laxative and effective for treatment of constipation.

They are also effective in curing sterility and increasing the libido and are helpful in preventing abdominal cancer. Dates are found to be effective in curing cardiovascular diseases too and can cure night blindness. **Did you know that date palm trees are the oldest cultivated trees in recorded history!**

DATE SYRUP (KHAJUR RAS)

Apart from having the properties of dates, date syrup is important as an alternative sweetening agent. It is used as it has a low GI and more medicinal value than artificial sweeteners.

DILL (SUVA)

Dill has calmative effects, greatly helping hiccups, hyperactivity and nervous disturbances. **An old wives' tale recommends boiling dill in wine and then inhaling the fumes to cure hiccups.** It also doubles up as a sedative, helping you have a good sleep. The essential oils present in it are stimulanting in nature and activate secretion of bile and digestive juices. As dill is a carminative, it greatly helps in expulsion and reduction of gases formed.

Dill is anti-congestive and anti-histaminic in nature, so it is helpful in respiratory disorders. It also helps maintain proper menstrual cycles.

FENNEL (SAUNF)

Fennel benefits the stomach and intestines, aids in digestion and stimulates the metabolism. Furthermore, fennel helps improve and cure problems related to irritable bowel syndrome (IBS) and the spleen, and also improves liver and kidney function.

Besides, the herb protects against cardiovascular disease and cancers (especially, estrogen-dependent cancer). The herb can be taken in the form of fennel tea too. It is also used to treat respiratory congestion, cough, bronchitis, sore throat, hoarseness in voice.

FENUGREEK (METHI)

Go to any home where there is a history of diabetes and you will spot a small katori of methi seeds which have been sprouted or soaked overnight at the breakfast table. **Fenugreek is a must for diabetics.**

Did you know that fenugreek also helps in improving digestive tract functions and should be regularly used as a cleansing agent? It is useful in the healing of different ulcers of the digestive tract. In chronic problems like ulcerative colitis, etc., fenugreek is claimed to provide a protective coating to the digestive tract, thus helping in providing relief. Fenugreek has a mild laxative property, which also helps cleaning toxins from the body, thus helping restoration from illness.

FIGS (ANJEER)

Many believe that it were figs that were actually the fruit in the Garden of Eden with Adam and Eve, not apples. Figs are excellent for a healthy bowel function due to the high levels of fibre. **Figs are among the most highly alkaline foods, making them useful in balancing the pH of the body, especially if you have an acidity problem and need to take antacids.** They are a good source of potassium, important in helping to regulate blood pressure. Also, a little known fact about figs is that they were presented as laurels to the winners in the earliest Olympics, making them the first 'medals' ever given!

FLAX (ALSI)

Flaxseed is the new wonder cure. Most frequently used as a laxative, flaxseed is also used for conditions such as high cholesterol, menopause, and breast cancer, among others because of its action on estrogen. Flaxseed lowers cholesterol by decreasing cholesterol absorption in the intestine. It also has beneficial effects on platelets, which cause blood-vessel clotting.

Flaxseed is extremely helpful during menopause and helps people with certain cancers that need estrogen to grow, such as breast cancer, because our body converts flaxseed into substances called lignan, which interferes with natural estrogen. **Two things to remember are that it can cause some stomach problems so it should be taken with a lot of water and should not be taken if bleeding problems exist.**

GARLIC (LASAN)

Garlic has a very extensive folk history of use in a broad range of ailments such as ringworm, candida, and vaginitis where it's parasitic, antiseptic, fungicidal, and tonic properties have proved to be useful. Externally, garlic juice is an excellent antiseptic for treating wounds. And it's strong smell should not serve as a deterrent to its use. **Did you know the smell of garlic can be removed while washing your hands under cold water while rubbing a stainless steel object?**

GINGER (ADRAK)

A must for Indian gravies, ginger is a classic tonic for the digestive tract. It stimulates digestion, and has the ability to prevent vomiting. It also tends to boost the pumping action of heart. Ginger protects the stomach from damaging effects of alcohol and non-steriodal, anti-inflammatory drugs, and may help prevent ulcers. It is also used as relief for sore throats if it is added to warm water and used to gargle with.

GHEE

Ghee is used to help with ulcers, constipation, and the promotion of healthy eyes and skin. It is said to be good for increasing memory and is said to balance the mind and enhance brain function. It is used for the treatment of burns and blisters. **The linolenic acid present in it helps in weight loss especially the belly fat, which greatly reduces risk of certain types of cancers and heart conditions.** Ghee is rich with antioxidants and acts as an aid in the absorption of vitamins and minerals from other foods and strengthens the immune system.

GUGGUL

Guggul has a wide range of applications, beginning with its use in treating rheumatic and arthritic pains and obesity. In addition, it treats a sluggish liver, malaria, nervous diseases, bronchial congestion, cardiac and circulatory problems, weak digestion, fractures, gynaecological problems, leucorrhoea, sterility, impotence, sexually transmitted diseases (STDs), and various skin diseases including acne and psoriasis. **It is also known to stimulate the libido as it has warming, circulatory properties.**

It is bitter to taste, which helps stimulate a good appetite and relieves gas and bloating. Guggul is a uterine stimulant, which makes it useful for regulating menstruation but it is generally stopped during pregnancy.

HONEY (SHAHED)

Honey is considered as the ambrosia of the gods and some ancient stories even refer it as 'liquid gold'. Honey contains sugars which are quickly absorbed by the digestive system and converted into energy; this can be used as instant energizer. As it is hygroscopic it speeds up healing of worn out tissue, increases growth of the healing tissue and dries up infected tissue. Honey acts as a sedative and is very useful in bed-wetting disorders.

A very good antioxidant, it restores damaged skin, making it look soft and young. It also has antibacterial properties due to its acidic nature and enzymatically produced hydrogen peroxide. It has the ability to stop hiccups, cure worm and urinary infections, diarrhoea, vomiting, and nausea. It may also be used to cleanse and heal wounds.

INDIAN GINSENG (ASHWAGANDHA)

The roots of ashwagandha have been found to be very useful in the treatment of rheumatic pain, inflammation of joints, nervous disorders, and epilepsy. A tonic of dried roots is very effective in case of hiccups, cold, and cough. **Ashwagandha is also known to improve the female reproductive system.** It also helps in the treatment of Alzheimer's and Parkinson's diseases, memory loss, and insomnia.

It is highly effective in treating neurological disorders, inflammations and anxiety. It improves sexual stamina along with sperm quality and count. It is a brilliant uterine tonic, which also enhances female libido. It also increases haemoglobin in the blood, and is helpful in the treatment of arthritis, asthma, leprosy, paralysis, and hypertension, and is effective to combat insomnia.

Did you know that the fruits of ashwagandha can be used as a substitute for the coagulation of milk in the process of cheese making?

JAGGERY (GUR)

Jaggery plays an omniscient role in Indian ceremonies as a sweetmeat. **In many Gujarati communities, the engagement is commonly known as 'gol-dhana', which literally means jaggery and coriander seeds!** Gur is used to treat anaemia, frequent muscle cramps, tension, or soreness. It is also taken during pregnancy and PMS. It relaxes the muscles and improves overall blood circulation. It is effective in reducing bloating and water retention. It is used to treat colds and reduce high blood pressure.

LIME (NIMBU)

The health benefits of lime include urinary disorders, skin care, respiratory disorders, relief from constipation, weight loss, eye care, improves digestion, healing of scurvy, piles, peptic ulcer, gout, gums, etc. It is a good appetizer and digestive. It helps to cure arthritis, rheumatism, early stage prostrate and colon cancer, cholera, arteriosclerosis, diabetes, fatigue, heart diseases, and even very high fever.

MACE (JAVITRI)

Did you know that mace is the outer lacy orange red covering of the nutmeg? It takes 400 pounds of nutmeg to produce one pound of mace. Mace is popularly used in several traditional cures for gastrointestinal disorders, malaria, and measles. It is also used in combination with other herbs as an aphrodisiac and galactagogue (lactation stimulant). **Apart from this, mace is chewed to prevent halitosis.**

MANGO POWDER (AMCHUR)

Raw mango powder or amchur is acidic, astringent, and anti-scorbutic in nature. Amchur also has high iron content, so pregnant women and people suffering from anaemia are counselled to eat it regularly. It fights acidity and improves digestion. Mangoes contain phenols, and phenolic compounds have potent antioxidant and anti-cancer properties. It is a superior source of Vitamins A and E, which helps hormonal system function proficiently. **Scurvy treatment is done with the help of mango powder.** Raw mango power is effective in relieving clogged pores of the skin. Also note, the next time you want to add a tangy flavour to your curry or chutney, a pinch of amchur will do the trick.

MARJORAM (KUTHARA)

During the Middle Ages, magical properties were attributed to the plant: it was thought to drive away spirits, imps, and witches and to render spells and curses ineffective. When taken in moderation, it helps in relieving menstruation pain and leucorrhoea. Since it increases menstruation flow the herb should not be taken during pregnancy and in heavy and prolonged menstrual periods. Essential oils in the marjoram herb have also been found to have antifungal and antibacterial functions. Sweet marjoram tea helps relieve nausea, flatulence, and is thought to have mild antiseptic functions. **Did you know that marjoram was dedicated to Aphrodite, the goddess of love, who is supposed to have created the potent little healing plant while in a state of perfect happiness?**

Melon Seeds (Magaz)

Originally thought to be from the Middle East, melon seeds were transported to the Americas by Columbus and the Spanish explorers. Melon seeds are a good source of dietary fibres, which is essential for healthy bowel movement and digestion. **Nutrients in these seeds are said to prevent cancer, improve and/or prevent cardiovascular disease, hypertension, and reduce levels of bad cholesterol.**

Mint (Pudina)

Mint was no doubt one of the earliest herbs discovered. It has been found in Egyptian tombs dating back to 1000 BC and has been part of the Chinese pharmacopoeia even longer.

Mint acts as an analgesic (topical), and also has anti-inflammatory, antiulcer properties. It also helps in dissolving gall stones, eliminating heartburn, improving solubility of bile, increasing bile acid and lecithin levels in the gall bladder. It inhibits and kills micro-organisms (Candida albicans, Herpes simplex, Influenza A viruses, Mumps virus, etc., inhibiting constipation, diarrhoea, and hyper contractility of the intestinal smooth muscle; serves as a mild anaesthetic to the stomach wall. Moreover, mint normalizes gastrointestinal activity, prevents congestion of blood to the brain, reduces bile cholesterol levels, stimulates circulation and contractile activity, and last but not the least, bile secretion in the gall bladder. Also, mint is a wonderful addition to lemonade.

MOLASSES (GUR RAS)

Molasses promotes the healing of wounds and also binds with toxins in the colon to fight against colon cancer. The calcium in molasses also helps to develop and maintain healthy bones and teeth. Bone problems occurring during menopause can also be prevented. **Consumption of molasses can help with a number of menstruation and menopausal symptoms such as PMS, cramping, mood swings, and hot flashes.** It is believed that molasses consumption can also reduce the size of fibroid tumours.

NUTMEG (JAIPHAL)

Nutmeg is a small package with several big benefits. Medically, nutmeg has strong antibacterial properties. It is effective in killing a number of cavity-causing bacteria in the mouth.

Alzheimer's is promoted by a certain enzyme in the brain. Myristicin in nutmeg inhibits production of that enzyme therefore preventing Alzheimer's and improves memory.

It is used in small dosages to reduce flatulence, aid digestion, and improve appetite. Nutmeg can help to combat asthma. It is also used to relax muscles. **Scary fact: in very**

large quantities, nutmeg has hallucinogenic effects. So, careful there!

ONION SEEDS (KALONJI)

These seeds, which have been used medicinally for at least 3,000 years, find a mention in the Bible, were found in King Tut's tomb, and used by Cleopatra and Nefertiti for beautification! Onion seeds are used to treat ailments including asthma, bronchitis, rheumatism, and related inflammatory diseases. **Its oil has been used to treat skin conditions such as eczema and boils and to treat cold symptoms.** It normalizes the secretions of the stomach and pancreas. This is very effective in the treatment of diabetes. It removes mucus obstruction of any part of the lungs, expels the gases, and strengthens the stomach.

OREGANO

All of us have that one friend who always asks for extra oregano from the delivery guy. It is renowned for being the most favourite pizza topping. **Oregano is used for indigestion, bloating, flatulence, coughs, urinary problems, bronchial problems, headaches, swollen glands, and to promote menstruation.** It has also been used to relieve fevers, diarrhoea, vomiting, and jaundice. Apart from this, oregano is used to relieve pain from rheumatism, swelling, itching, aching muscles, and sores.

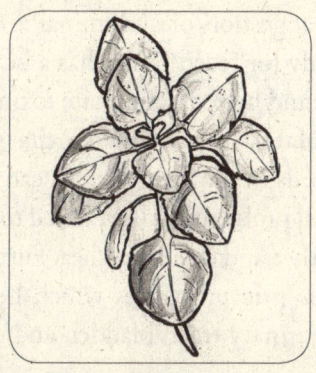

PAPRIKA

Paprika is used for relieving colds, fever, and headaches. Because it causes the eyes and nose to run, it helps to relieve congestion. **Paprika is useful for treating obesity.** It also affects the breakdown of carbohydrates in the diet, thereby keeping blood sugar levels from fluctuating widely after meals. It is beneficial in helping to control diabetes. Paprika is used to boost the immune system. It can also ease sore throats and stop constant coughs.

PARSLEY

Did you know that parsley is regularly used as the equivalent of dhaniya in Indian cuisine abroad? Parsley is recommended as a natural cure for bladder problems, prostate or kidney. Parsley root is a diuretic that has been used for various forms of dropsy (abnormal accumulation of fluid in body tissues or a body cavity), congestion of abdominal viscera, etc. It acts as a natural remedy for fever. It also has a beneficial effect on blood circulation and helps to eliminate toxins from the body.

Parsley stimulates blood flow in the pelvic area and uterus. Parsley seeds in the form of a tea can be used to helps improve menstrual problems. It has proved to be very effective in curing amenorrhea and dysmenorrhea. Furthermore, parsley has amazing antiseptic properties which help it purify the digestive system, urinary tract, bladder, and uterus.

PEPPERCORNS (KALI MIRCH)

One sneeze, and there comes your grandmom with a kali mirch-shahad decoction. Traditionally, black pepper has been used to treat the common cold and upper respiratory tract infections. Black pepper is used for digestive disorders, such as indigestion, vomiting, diarrhoea, and flatulence. **It promotes proper urination and sweating that helps get rid of harmful toxins from the body.** It also helps in constipation, ear ache, gangrene, heart disease, hernia, insect bites, insomnia, joint pain, liver and lung disease, sunburn, and toothaches. It is not to be used by patients who are going to have or have recently had abdominal surgery.

PINE NUTS (CHILGOZA)

Pine nuts are nature's only source of pinolenic acid, which stimulates hormones and helps diminish appetite. They have the highest concentration of oleic acid and helps protect the heart. They also help alleviate muscle cramps, tension, and fatigue. These nuts help protect the skin from dryness. **A cooking tip for you: pesto sauce is prepared by making a blend of garlic, basil, olive oil, and pine nuts.** Give it a try it.

PISTACHIOS (PISTA)

Pistachios are one of the oldest flowering nut trees, and are one of the only two nuts mentioned in the Bible. **Humans have been consuming pistachios for more than 9000 years!** Pistachios greatly reduce risks of heart disease. Antioxidant-rich pistachio eases the effects of daily stress, contributes to the reduction of inflammation, a root cause of many diseases, as well as oxidation by free radicals. This super nut blunts the impact of carbohydrates on blood sugar.

POMEGRANATE SEEDS (ANAARDANA)

Pomegranate seed oil adds moisture, has natural oestrogenic properties, boasts antioxidants, is anti-inflammatory and antimicrobial, improves skin elasticity, and protects the skin. **It provides relief from minor skin irritations and inflammation, including dry skin, eczema, psoriasis, and sunburned skin.** Pomegranate seeds are rich in specific polyphenols, such as tannins, quercetin, and anthocyanins—all of which may offer both heart health and anti-cancer benefits.

POPPY SEEDS (KHUS KHUS)

In the sweltering hot summers, it's common to serve a refreshing glass of khus sherbet as a welcoming drink. Khus khus has anti-inflammatory and antiseptic effects that provide relief from inflammations in the circulatory and nervous systems. This also has a good curing effect on gout, arthritis, rheumatism, and other bone-related diseases. **The oil obtained from khus khus has a sedative effect and aids in the treatment of emotional outbursts, such as anger, anxiety, epileptic and hysteric attacks, restlessness, nervousness, etc.**

PRUNES (SUKHA ALUBUKHARA)

Prunes promote good digestive health. Prunes make great filling snacks, and can help curb weight gain. **They also are known to prevent heart disease and can lower cholesterol levels.** The potassium and antioxidants in prunes is essential in reducing high blood pressure, preventing atherosclerosis and in prunes fighting free radicals and ageing. Buy some pitted prunes. It's like fat-free candy and, of course, super healthy!

PUMPKIN SEEDS (KADDU KE BEEJ)

Back in the day, the rich would use slivers of pistachio as garnish for mithai while the poor would have to make do with pumpkin seeds. Pumpkin seeds promote overall prostate health and alleviate difficult urination associated with an enlarged prostate. **They are also useful for treatment of depression.** Because they are high in zinc, pumpkin seeds are a natural protector against osteoporosis. They work wonders in lowering cholesterol and in addition are used as a natural cure for tapeworms and parasites.

QUINOA

Quinoa, the 'miracle grain of the Andes', in its wholegrain form, may be effective in preventing and treating artherosclerosis, breast cancer, diabetes and insulin resistance. It is close to one of the most complete foods in nature because it contains amino acids, enzymes, vitamins and minerals, fibre, antioxidants, and phytonutrients. Quinoa acts as a prebiotic that feeds the microflora (good bacteria) in the intestines. It is easily digested for optimal absorption of nutrients. **Quinoa is gluten-free and safe for those with gluten intolerance and people on a celiac diet.** The body ecology programme is gluten free and casein free. It decreases the craving for processed foods.

RAISINS (KISHMISH)

Ask people to include dry fruits in their daily diet and the finicky eaters will only say yes to the tastiest ones: raisins. The health benefits of raisins include relief from constipation, acidosis, anaemia, fever, and sexual weakness. Raisins are known to be helpful in bone health, eye care, weight gain, and dental care. They also increase sexual desire by stimulating the libido and inducing arousal. They are beneficial for the lungs, brain, throat, the bowel, and the womb. People who have a frail respiratory system can advantage greatly from regular eating of raisins. It also makes the brain sharp and helps in balancing emotions. **They are also advantageous for women who want to conceive, as they are known to increase natural fertility.**

ROSEMARY

You must have seen bottles of rosemary bath oil during your last visit to the spa. That is because it has a relaxing and soothing effect on your skin and body. **It can be used as a tonic and**

pick-me-up when feeling nervous, mentally tired, depressed, etc. The plant is rich in volatile oils, flavanoids, and phenolic acids, which are strongly antiseptic and anti-inflammatory. Rosmarinic acid present in rosemary has properties to treat toxic shock syndrome. And to top it, it adds just wonderful flavour to your pasta.

SAFFRON (KESAR)

Saffron is one of the most expensive spices; buying just 5 gm of kesar will burn a hole in your pocket. But be careful from where you buy it: dealers have often fooled buyers by selling coloured stamen instead of the real deal. Saffron is used to treat mild or moderate depression. **Saffron is taken at bedtime, usually in tea or milk, to treat insomnia.** It is also helpful in treating asthma by clearing the airways to aid breathing.

Saffron also acts as an antioxidant and stimulates blood circulation, which prevents hardening of the arteries.

Carotenoids in saffron help fight various cancers, like leukaemia and sarcoma. Women use saffron to induce menstruation and to take care of painful periods.

SHATAVRI

Shatavari is perhaps best known as a female rejuvenative. An interesting fact about the etymology of the word 'shatavri' is that it means 'the wife of 100', which refers to the reproductive strength of women who take it. **It is useful for infertility, decreased libido, threatened miscarriage, menopause, leucorrhoea and has the ability to balance the pH in the cervical area.** Dry membranes, like those on the vaginal wall, are also brought into equilibrium through the herbs' demulcent action.

Men also benefit from the herb, as it assists in the treatment of impotence and general sexual debility. In addition, shatavari is also quite effective for stomach ulcers, hyperacidity, and diarrhoea.

SPELT

This ancient grain is a cousin of wheat, and is a great help to people who are intolerant of its poor cousin. Spelt is highly soluble in water therefore helps the body absorbing nutrients and improving digestion. It is high in protein (considerably higher than wheat), higher in B complex vitamins, and high in both simple and complex carbohydrates. These complex carbohydrates are a significant factor in blood clotting and stimulating the body's immune system. Spelt is also a superb fibre resource. **It can help with migraine, lower risk of Type II diabetes, cardiovascular disease, and help women avoid gall stones and breast cancer.**

STAR ANISE (STAR PHOOL)

With the distinction of being the prettiest spice, star anise is native to Vietnam and southern China. It improves memory, gets rid of oily skin, calms coughs, boosts milk production for nursing mothers, and acts as a natural antacid. It is very effective as a carminative. It is also used as a cough remedy and to treat bronchitis and asthma. In addition, it is also used for relieving menopausal discomforts, and for treating prostate cancer in men. It definitely has potential in treating hepatitis and cirrhosis.

Sunflower Seeds (Suryamukhi ke beej)

We generally buy sunflower seeds to feed the birds. What we don't realize is that we should feed it to ourselves too (only the shelled ones by the way)! **Sunflower seed are used as a medicine to ease chest pain, decrease water retention, expel worms, improve eyesight, and provide energy.** The seeds helps lower blood pressure. Because they are high in potassium and low in sodium, they act as a diuretic. They help improve cardiovascular health, suppress allergic reactions, and help people quit smoking.

Tamarind (Imli)

Tamarind is so sour that Marco Polo claimed the Malabar pirates made their victims swallow a mixture of tamarind and sea water, forcing them to vomit the entire contents of their stomach, revealing any pearls they may have swallowed to conceal them! Tamarind is used for treating a variety of medical conditions including colds, constipation, liver problems, gall bladder ailments, fever, nausea during

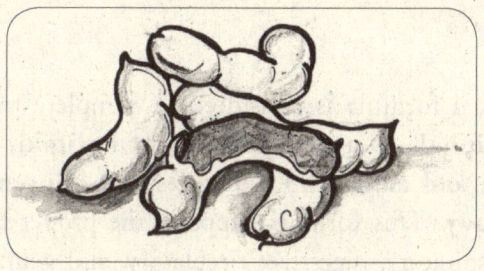

pregnancy, intestinal parasites, and stomach complaints. It is applied to the skin as a dense paste to make a cast for broken bones. Tamarind seed extract is also used in eye solutions to treat symptoms of dry eyes.

TRIKATU

Trikatu is an ayurvedic compound which contains black pepper, long pepper, and ginger in equal proportions. It behaves as a digestive powder and anti-mucus, thereby improving gastric and respiratory functions. It heats up the internal organs and revives weak organ functions. As an aphrodisiac, trikatu strengthens reproductive functions, warming, and energizing the organs. Trikatu is a safe digestive stimulant and expectorant.

Trikatu is used internally in the treatment of gastric and abdominal disorders, asthma, bronchitis, coughs, dysentery, pyrexia, and insomnia. **One reason why trikatu should be your new best friend is that it is considered to assist weight loss, as it maximizes metabolism and balances blood glucose to actually reduce food cravings!**

TRIPHALA

This herbal formula is considered a complete remedy in itself. **Triphala is a combination of haritaki, behara/ vibhitaki and amla, and detoxifies and rejuvenates the whole body.** This formula supports the proper functions of the respiratory, digestive, circulatory, and genitourinary systems. It is also used in treating haemorrhages, epistaxis, and many other gynaecological disorders. Triphala supports healthy digestion, absorption, and gently maintains regularity of bowel movement. It is a very good natural antioxidant and assists natural internal cleansing. Triphala is also very useful in eye disorders (a combination of triphala, honey and castor oil improves vision). The herbal powder is the preferred choice in case of anaemia as it increases the haemoglobin and red blood cell count. It is a potent immunity builder.

TURKISH APRICOTS (TURKI KHURMANI)

In Shakespeare's *A Midsummer Night's Dream*, apricots are mentioned to be aphrodisiacs. Apricots are used orally for infertility, eye inflammation, intestinal spasms, to expel intestinal worms and parasites, and prevent gall stones, and vaginal infections. **Apricot is highly valued as a gentle laxative, which is beneficial in the treatment of constipation due to its insoluble fibre and soluble fibre, pectin.** The fruit provides bulk, helping to keep bowel movement regular, balances the pH level in the intestines, and binds toxins for removal from the body.

TURMERIC (HALDI)

Haven't you wondered how brides always have such glowing skin? The secret is haldi. Every Indian bride goes through a ritualistic bath with haldi, sandalwood paste, and rose water.

Turmeric has a range of benefits, which include its powerful anti-inflammatory abilities which researchers believe make it a cure for arthritis and joint stiffness, and even Alzheimer's.

Turmeric is extremely helpful in curing common colds, healing wounds, infections of the liver, and is even used as a blood purifier. It acts as an antiseptic for small scratches and burns, as it has the ability to fight bacteria. This spice is useful in aiding digestive tract and circulatory system problems along with being an antioxidant.

THYME (AJMA)

Chefs always recommend thyme for meat marinades. **It tenderizes and aromatizes meat.** Apart from that, thyme has an antioxidant effect; thus regular use of this herb improves the health and longevity of individual body cells prolonging the life of the body. The plant possesses remarkable respiratory properties, which help internal cures of dry coughs, whooping coughs, bronchitis, asthma, brochial catarrah, laryngitis, indigestion, diarrhoea and enuresis in children. Externally, it is also used to treat gums, rheumatism, fungal infections, arthritis, and tonsillitis. It should not be prescribed to pregnant women under any condition though.

WALNUTS (AKHROT)

Walnuts are used medicinally for parasite infections, diphtheria, and syphilis. They can be used to cure skin problems such as acne, eczema, inflammation, and wounds. Additional uses include digestive disorders, colitis, haemorrhoids, tonsillitis, and thyroid disease. **Regular consumption of walnuts helps in lowering cholesterol levels, controlling high blood sugars, and improving cardiovascular functions.** In Greek culture, walnuts were called *karyon* which means 'head' as the shell looks like a human skull and the kernel itself resembles a human brain!

SUPERFOODS. WHAT ARE THEY?

Junk food, take out, fast food, microwaveable food, reducing the amount of our physical exertion to next to nothing. You name it, all of us will have them on our 'Not to Do' list.

While all of this does sound ominous, fortunately we have solutions at hand. There are certain, almost magical, foods, which are abundant in vitamins, minerals, and other nutrients while remaining 100 percent natural. They are often called functional foods by scientists, but are also known as 'superfoods' by the layperson.

These superfoods, in conjunction with a healthy lifestyle, may be used to help meet a variety of goals, such as losing weight, becoming fitter and healthier, or preventing and treating a whole host of diseases and conditions.

So, don't wait for Superman. These superfoods are here to help. Here are a few important ones.

BEE POLLEN

Bee pollen could be the next big superstar. It's a relatively inexpensive food, which contains well over 28 minerals, 11 enzymes and co-enzymes, over a dozen different vitamins, antioxidants, and 14 fatty acids. **The specialty of bee pollen is that it has many nutrients in a miniscule package with very less calories and no fat!** Scientists have also observed that the addition of bee pollen to a person's diet results in a dramatic reduction in blood triglyceride and bad cholesterol.

Daily consumption results in prevention of erratic outbreaks of allergic reactions from regular pollen, spores, dust and other environmental allergies.

The immune system is greatly boosted by Vitamin C and E, which are present in sufficient quantities in pollen. Its ability to boost the immune system comes from the unique blend of flower nectar, honey, and the bee's own enzymes, and has also been proven in scientific trials to help prevent the development of cancerous tumours.

Bee pollen also acts as a very good antioxidant and rejuvenates skin and protects against ageing.

BLACK COHOSH

Black cohosh is a tall perennial plant in the buttercup family that grows in eastern and central areas of the United States. **It is one of the more popular herbal remedies for menopausal symptoms, such as hot flashes, night sweats, migraines, mood disturbances, heart palpitations and vaginal dryness,**

as well as for menstrual cramps and bloating. Black cohosh is generally considered to be very well tolerated by the body, with few, if any, side effects—though everyone's different, and some women report mild GI problems when taking it.

DONG QUAI

Dong Quai, the other name of which being Chinese Angelica, is mainly renowned for its uses in treating women's problems, which include a low libido, the problems of menopause, cramps, PMS, and is also particularly helpful in getting rid of hot flashes and menstrual cramps. It is extensively used as an aphrodisiac. It is also used as a liver tonic and in treating sciatica and shingles.

It has been used by the Chinese for more than two thousand years as a strengthener of the heart, lung, spleen, liver, and kidney meridians, and as a tonic for the blood. **Remember: do not consume this herb during pregnancy or menstruation (it will increase menstrual blood flow if taken during the days when you are bleeding) or for people taking blood-thinning agents.**

GUARANA POWDER

Paullinia cupana, better known as guarana, is a plant native to Brazil and the Amazon Basin. Guarana is primarily used to boost energy. It has two times more caffeine than coffee beans, with its content rate at 2 to 5 percent.

Guarana can improve memory and alertness. In many

cases it can also improve a person's mood. The biggest advantage—and one that most people aren't aware of—is that it can help you lose weight. It also has antioxidant and antibacterial effects. People with predisposed heart conditions should consult the doctor before using it. It's also wise to use caution if you experience heart palpitations after taking guarana.

MACA

Maca is a cruciferous root found growing in the high regions of Peru and has been cultivated for about 2000 years. The Peruvians believe it gives strength and endurance, enhances ones fertility, and supports pregnancies.

The maca root helps balance the body's delicate endocrine system and also enables a person to cope with stress. It energizes naturally, and can assist in the reproductive function by balancing hormones and increasing fertility. It also improves memory and helps combat anaemia. One of the very interesting things about maca is that it is an adaptogen herb, i.e. the herb will work on the body according to the needs, age, and gender of the person using it. Maca is very safe even if taken in large dosages for there are no known adverse side effects of maca.

MORINGA POWDER

The moringa tree's nutrient-rich leaves contain more Vitamin C than an orange, more calcium than a glass of milk, more potassium than a banana, and more iron than a serving of spinach. Still not convinced? **Let's put it this way, eating a serving of moringa can save you the trouble of eating several pounds worth of vegetables to get the same level of nutrition.**

Among its many health benefits, moringa is very powerful immune system booster. Moringa is one of the richest natural food sources of zinc, beta-carotene, and Vitamin E, making it a convenient and ideal food for maintaining great eyesight. Moringa acts as a great natural sleeping aid. One of the often-overlooked benefits of moringa is its ability to boost a person's brain development and help people maintain mental clarity over prolonged periods of time.

Moringa is a great anti-cancer food as it not only helps fight tumours, it prevents their formation in the first place.

It also has been proven to aid in treatment of an array of hepatic diseases such as cirrhosis of the liver, acute or chronic, degeneration of the liver and scarring caused due to alcohol and drug abuse. This is because moringa not only stops the toxicity that causes these diseases, but also helps *reverse* it. **Moringa accelerates the regeneration process of the liver by about four times the normal speed, eventually helping the liver regain full functionality.** Apart from all of this, (yes there is more!) moringa is undoubtedly one of the most powerful all-natural anti-ageing foods available today.

Also, because moringa is an all-natural food product and not a medicine, it is completely safe to consume, whether the person eating it is 90 years old or nine months old.

RED CLOVER

Red clover is used to battle hot flashes, PMS, improve breast health and size, urine production, and blood circulation. Furthermore, it helps prevent osteoporosis, reduces chances of internal blood clots and reduces risks of benign prostate hyperplasia.

Red clover may also block enzymes thought to contribute to prostate cancer in men. It is believed that red clover may help to prevent heart disease in several ways. In addition, red clover may also promote an increase in the secretion of bile acid. It has been found to be helpful in quitting smoking.

ST JOHN'S WORT

St John's Wort is one of the most commonly used herbs in the US. **It was named because the flowers were said to bloom for the first time around June 24, the birthday of St John the Baptist.** This plant is as effective as tricyclic antidepressants for the short-term treatment (one to three months) of mild to moderate depression. Some alternative practitioners recommend it for ear pain caused due to ear infection. St John's Wort has been used to cure menopausal mood swings and premenstrual syndromes as well.

SPIRULINA

Spirulina is a form of blue-green algae that usually grows on the surface of lakes and ponds. It was first harvested by

Mesoamerican civilizations many centuries ago, yet only rediscovered about forty years ago. It provides some of the best nutrition available in one convenient package. **It's one of the best non-animal sources of protein available, and it also contains every essential amino acid our body needs to grow, heal, and develop.**

Spirulina contains significant amounts of phycocyanin, chlorophyll, and spirulan, which help inhibit the growth of cancer colonies. It also contains a wide variety of essential fatty acids, which are essential for maintaining good blood cholesterol levels while also maintaining good cardiovascular and brain health. Those of you who continue to crinkle your noses at the thought of this algae, spirulina has been declared by the UN as the 'best food for the future'. Stock it up people!

GOJI BERRIES

Grown in the temperate and sub-tropical regions of China, Mongolia and in the in the Himalayas in Tibet, this small bright red coloured berry is packed with nutrients and essential vitamins. The herbalists in China, Tibet and India have been using goji berries for over 6000 years to correct bad eyesight and protect the liver. It is also used to improve sexual function and fertility. These little red berries boost immune function, improve circulation, promote longevity, and strengthen the legs.

Add about 1.4 cups of dried goji berries to low-fat yoghurt and fruits of your choice and blend to a smoothie that will keep you active and energetic all morning long.

Being calorie dense, goji berries can be incorporated into a weight-loss programme or as a meal replacement by eliminating the bulk. **They contain more beta carotene than carrots.** They also have more antioxidant power than any other known food source.

BERRY ENERGY GREEN SMOOTHIE RECIPE

Ingredients

1 medium banana, peeled
1 kiwi, peeled
⅓ cup goji berries
¼ cup raw cacao nibs (or ⅛ cup cacao powder)
1 stalk of celery, chopped
1 cup fresh parsley, chopped

1 cup fresh baby spinach, chopped

6 to 8 ounces of water (or coconut water)

2 to 3 ice cubes to chill if desired

1 scoop hemp or rice protein powder (optional)

Preparation

❖ Start by adding the liquid to your blender (I use a Vitamix), followed by the soft fruit.

❖ Add the greens to your blender in the end.

❖ Blend on high for 30 seconds or until the smoothie is creamy.

Note: If you do not have a high-speed blender, grind cacao nibs in a coffee grinder or use cacao powder and be sure to soak the goji berries in water for 10 minutes before adding them to your blender.

3

Restoring Balance: Techniques for Cleansing and Purification

SOHAIL, A HALE AND HEARTY GUY, CAME TO ME WITH THE complaint of feeling unwell all the time. He claimed he lacked energy, even after eight hours of sleep. He felt like his food wasn't being digested and woke up with a terrible burning sensation in his chest. There were times when he would burp and taste his previous meal. He also had blinding headaches. I asked him to do his blood work and the results came back normal. I immediately asked him the most important question: what was his dietary recall?

As it happened, Sohail was used to drinking at least six cups of black coffee a day, eating meat all the time, and drinking very little water. He used to take long gaps between his meals, and rarely ate dinner before 10 pm. All of these were the indicators of acidosis. The first thing I asked him to do was to get his pH checked. He did and voila! His pH was 5.3, which is really quite high on the acidic chart. Apart from changing his diet (read on to see the important dietary elements to curb acidosis), I also asked him to put parsley, mint, and celery into his drinking water, eat ten black raisins on waking up, and have small meals at regular intervals. Two months later, his pH was back to a balanced 7.5.

So, what is this pH that caused so much harm in an apparently healthy man and why is it so important to take proper dietary measures to ensure that the pH stays within the prescribed limit? Read ahead to learn more about pH and its importance in bodily functions.

WHAT IS PH?

pH is a central measurable parameter of our body's well being, like BP, blood sugar, and cholesterol levels. We owe the concept of pH to Danish chemist SPL Sørensen, who introduced it in 1909. The pH scale takes its name from the words: **potential of hydrogen**. It is a scale used to measure the acidity or alkalinity of a solution. The pH scale uses a range from 0 to 14, with 7.0 indicating neutrality. Numbers beginning at 7.0 and moving towards 0 signify acidity, while the numbers beginning at 7.0 and moving towards 14 signify alkalinity, so the scale divides acids from bases.

There are several categorizations for solutions as measured by the pH scale. A common one is this:

pH 0 - 2	Strongly acidic
pH 3 - 5	Weakly acidic
pH 6 - 8	Neutral
pH 9 - 11	Weakly basic
pH 12 - 14	Strongly basic

It is only when the pH levels are balanced that we have a revitalized body and more mental clarity. This is when the body starts functioning to the best of its biochemical ability. To maintain this optimum health, our body fluids and tissues must remain slightly alkaline, i.e. at a pH of 7.352.

Sadly this never happens because practically all metabolic processes that take place in our body, right from breathing to digesting food to producing energy all create by-products which are acidic in nature. Hence, our body is forever striving to maintain that delicate acid–base balance. **When our body is acidic our health is compromised and our susceptibility to diseases and infections increases.** We gain weight, become stressed, have difficulty in falling asleep at night, suffer from aching muscles, lack energy, and are prone to coughs and colds, nasal congestion, irritability, anxiety, and panic attacks.

Moreover, if you are already suffering from some disease, and the pH of your body fluids is acidic (less than 7), then this in turn will further increase inflammation, degeneration of soft tissues, and bone mineral loss. Your body will break down bones for its calcium, which will be used as a buffer to neutralize the acid levels. The scary thing is that at a pH of 7.2, the body maintains the levels of minerals already present in the bones while at a pH of 7.4, your body will start to build bone by diverting more calcium and other minerals into the bones.

Your body must maintain a balance between acid and alkaline to function properly. Acidosis, which occurs when your blood pH falls below 7.35, can affect your central nervous system and lead to a coma. Severe acidosis can be fatal. Alkalosis, or blood-pH levels above 7.45, can lead to muscle spasms and convulsions, which can also cause death.

A LITTLE FACT ABOUT BODY pH

Did you know when a person has cancer, his body pH is 1,000 times lesser than an average person's body pH? Cancer tumours thrive in an acidic body.

ARE YOU ACIDIC OR ALKALINE?

Test the pH level of your saliva, which is typically more acidic than blood. Normal results should be between 6.5 and 6.8. Your saliva should be tested at least one hour before or two hours after eating.

Urine might not be as accurate as saliva for testing pH, as levels can fluctuate dramatically during the day for example: a morning sample should be between 6.0 and 6.5, but a sample afterwards in the day can be between 6.5 and 7.0 and still be pronounced as acceptable.

It is very important to understand that a food's acid or alkaline-forming tendency in the body has nothing to do with the actual pH of the food itself. Very often a client will tell me that he or she has severe heartburn, particularly after eating a hearty steak or drinking a glass of wine the night before. Meat is considered as an alkaline food as it has a pH above 7 on the pH scale. In order to maintain the slightly alkaline nature of the body fluids, our body makes a lot more acid while digesting and assimilating the nutrients from that piece of meat. That is the reason for the hyperacidity. If I recommend a few sips of lemon juice to someone who has hyperacidity they look aghast! **Lemons are very acidic but after digestion they leave an alkaline residue, hence reducing the heartburn.**

Breakfast is the most important meal of the day. What you eat at this meal will go a long way in energizing you. However, if you need your daily fix of caffeine at this meal, do not wonder why you spend the rest of your day looking for antacids. Coffee, white bread, jam, and milk are all acid-forming foods. A better breakfast option would be wholewheat toasts or fresh fruit and yoghurt which are neutral foods.

The best breakfast option would be some herbal tea, five soaked almonds, the alkalizing green smoothie (recipe given below), and a small bowl of steamed sprouts, all of which are alkaline forming foods.

GREEN SMOOTHIE

This green smoothie keeps the pH of your body fluids slightly alkaline.

Ingredients

25 spinach leaves
1 tsp wheatgrass powder
2 dates
Juice of 1 sour lime
1 banana
1 apple or pear
1 pinch turmeric powder
200 ml water

Preparation

❖ Blend all the ingredients together.
❖ Consume as soon as you've made it.

STRIKING THE BALANCE

The body is at its healthiest when it's slightly alkaline; that is, the blood pH level is somewhere around 7.35. However, many of the foods we eat every day are highly acidic and lacking in nutrients, which can cause an acidic pH balance. Your lifestyle will have to be modified very significantly if you want to lessen the effects that acidic foods have on the body. If you follow these few steps, and you will be able to prevent the threat of alkaline imbalance in your body.

Stay well hydrated: by drinking at least 2 to 2.5 litres a day, you keep your body flushed of toxins and help maintain an alkaline balance. Each time a client complains of acid reflux, the first thing I ask them is about their water consumption; 90 percent of the time they report that they have not been able to drink sufficient water.

> You can even add an alkaline supplement to your water for an added boost. If you cannot find one, just add a stalk of celery or twenty mint leaves to your bottle of water.

Eat highly alkaline foods: A healthy balanced is a diet that's 80 percent alkaline and 20 percent acidic. Examples of foods you can eat to bring your pH back into balance include avocado, garlic, asparagus, spinach, soy, tomatoes, radishes, and sprouts. Some fruits are neutral and are okay to eat in moderation.

Highly acidic foods should be avoided or eaten only moderately. Examples include most meats, cheese, artificial sweeteners, sugar, coffee, alcohol, and breads. When we eat foods that have a pH above 7, for example meat, then the body produces more acid in order to maintain a near-neutral/slightly alkaline pH of the body fluids. So now you know why you sometime suffer acid reflux/heartburn the morning after indulging in a sumptuous steak!

Be kind to your digestive tract: Instead of eating three big meals, eat five or six smaller ones. Thoroughly chew your food before swallowing and eat slowly. Make sure your diet is rich in fibre and take a probiotic supplement or eat a bowl of homemade yoghurt to maintain proper digestive health.

Reduce your stress level: because stress increases the acid level in your body.

I understand that all this is easy for me to say, which is why I ask my clients to place a strand of kesar on their tongues when things get bad.

It acts like a charm to calm you down. You should remember to take deep breaths whenever you feel that things are getting out of hand, and take the time to relax or mediate or whatever makes you feel less tense.

Exercise: Get as much of it as possible. A daily workout helps to keep the pH level in check and on the alkaline side. Trust me, that 30-minute workout will go a long way in being healthy.

I understand how difficult it is to modify our diets and lifestyles, especially in the fast-paced lives that we lead. Having said that, our health is more important than everything else. But

I also know that certain things cannot be avoided. Hardcore non-vegetarians cannot give up their meat. Hence, here are some tips about the different kinds of food and their alkaline contents, and the best way to combine them in your daily diet.

Green vegetables: are the best sources of high alkaline foods. Include celery, broccoli, and raw spinach to your diet and the high fibre, vitamins, minerals and low calories will work wonders. However, there are certain vegetables you should limit. Corn, navy beans, lentils, olives, lima beans, winter squash, kidney beans, pickles, sauerkraut, mushrooms, pinto beans, potatoes, watercress, artichokes, and asparagus all have a high acid content.

POTATO WONDER

Although the potato it is not a green vegetable, it has very high alkaline content, more than most vegetables. 'The potato's wealth of alkaline elements make it the best choice to counter the acidification of the body,' according to Christopher Vasey, author of the *Acid–Alkaline Diet for Optimum Health*.

Fruits: Some fruits are considered acidic. This does not mean you have to completely avoid them, but you should limit your consumption of these varieties. Acidic fruits include blackberries, blueberries, cranberries, plums, rhubarb, currants and prunes. Also keep in mind that canned fruits are a lot more acidic than fresh fruits. Some fruits like lemons, watermelon, limes and papayas, produce alkalinity in the body. Fruits, however, must be eaten by themselves to facilitate digestion. *The Tao of Detox* by Daniel Reid says fruit digestion is delayed when you eat fruit along with other food groups. If fruits sit in the stomach too long, it begins to ferment and release toxic acids. **Eating fruit in the morning is a better option because the stomach is empty.**

Almonds: If you're looking for a healthy snack in between meals, try almonds. These nuts are alkalizing to the body and a good source of calcium and magnesium. Choose only raw almonds.

Millets: Most grains are acid forming but millet is an exception. Millet is a tiny, round grain that can accompany a variety of meals. This grain can be prepared creamy, like mashed potatoes or fluffy, like rice. Millet can also be made into porridge. In the *The pH Balance Diet* Bharti Vyas and Suzanne Quesne say that millet contains no gluten so it is a good option for people who are gluten sensitive.

Grains: A variety of grains and grain products are considered acidic. You need to watch out for processed grains and baked goods as they are high in acid and low in fibre. These include cereal grains, white bread, bagels, pasta, doughnuts, white rice, pastries, crackers, etc. You should consume moderately acidic grains like oats, quinoa, buckwheat, wheat, rye and barley.

Animal products: High-protein animal products, such as beef, pork, seafood, fish, lamb, organ meat, turkey, veal, and venison, are highly acidic. Bacon, sausage, corned beef, and other processed meat products have the highest acidity and should only be consumed occasionally. Milk, ice cream, butter, eggs, and processed cheese are dairy products high in acid. Although these foods provide you with protein and calcium, their consumption should be kept to a minimum.

Fats and oils: are high in acid include butter, sesame oil, corn oil, sunflower oil, canola oil, lard, olive oil, flax oil, sunflower oil, avocado oil, and safflower oil. When these oils are cooked, they become acidifying. If using them on a salad as a dressing or as a dip for bread, they are less acidic.

Beverages: There are a variety of commonly consumed beverages, which are acidic in nature. Alcoholic beverages are acidic. Coffee, tea, and soft drinks are acidifying as well.

HERBS TO RESTORE BALANCE

Most of our Indian herbs and spices like ginger, garlic, tulsi, and coriander are alkalizing. Thyme, oregano, and rosemary can also add a flavour-packed alkalizing boost to your favourite foods and recipes. The alkalizing power of herbs can be increased by substituting acid forming coffee and tea with herbal tea.

Aloe vera juice restores pH balance, calms inflammation, provides antioxidants, and has a mild laxative effect. A number of other herbs are useful for cleaning the colon, liver, and kidneys, and alkalizing your system. Bell peppers, ginger, alfalfa, beets, flax seed, psyllium husk, oat bran, apples, pears, guavas, red and brown rice, saunf, and mint all help in restoring the pH balance.

Chilli peppers, turmeric, cinnamon, mustard and curry leaves are herbs high in mineral content, which helps balance pH and lessens the need for the body to use its mineral reserves, especially of calcium, to reduce the effect of a high acid diet.

Nature is renowned for balancing every odd with an even. Our bodies also need to be balanced in the same way. Our food, diet, the amount of stress we take, and the work we do all points towards the balance we have in life. You must have heard of 'all work and no play'? That is an imbalance too. As is, of course, all play and no work. The little steps we take in life lead to bigger decisions, and where those decisions will intersect, we can't foresee.

So, now you know why Sohail suffered, and how it was a simple matter of changing the diet to improve his health. The next time you suffer from extreme acidity during stressful conditions, remember it's the black coffee and the lack of water that are causing it. pH imbalance can lead to harsh symptoms and severe diseases.

Now, we move on to water therapy ideal for body cleansing and purification. And the best part is that, they're easy peasy lemon squeezy.

4

Water Cures

WHILE TAKING A DIETARY RECALL, I ALWAYS ASK PEOPLE ABOUT their water intake, and they tell me that they have not more than three glasses of water a day but they have five cups of tea/coffee, four glasses of juice/nimbu paani, and a glass of milk or buttermilk!

The difference between liquid intake and water intake is usually misunderstood. All liquids do not necessarily hydrate your system.

In a very drastic case, I once had a 17-year-old boy who was chronically constipated, had hyperacidity, and acne. He said he couldn't drink plain water, barely managed half a glass a day, but was very happy to report that his overall liquid consumption was very high. He proudly informed me that he was consuming three and half litres of liquid a day. When my eyebrows shot up, he clarified that he had two litres of coke, four cups of tea and three to four cups of coffee, apart from the odd glass of wine. I tried my best to explain that when the body needed to be hydrated, the best liquid is water. The caffeine in coffee, tea, and coke was dehydrating rather than hydrating his system. He refused to drink plain water, so I put him on a therapeutic decoction of mint, parsley, ginger, lime, and honey, all added to three litres of water. He loved the taste, saw the difference it made to his bowel movement, skin, and general health and now says he has been converted for life.

Water. It is one of the most important things that a human body needs to survive. So much so that your body actually has a drought management system which prevents dehydration and hence ensures your survival. Water makes up more than two-thirds of human body weight, and without water, we would die in around three to four days.

Did you know that even if there is a 2 percent drop in the body's water supply, it will cause basic dehydration symptoms: difficulty with basic math, inability to focus on small print like that of a computer screen and bad short term memory?

It is one of the most common causes of daytime fatigue.

Yes, we all know everything about water. Haven't we been learning about it since we were little kids in school? However, you'll be surprised to find the sheer number of people who have come to me with problems that stem from not drinking water. Dehydration affects our body in many ways, all of them bad.

Water acts as a lubricant in digestion and almost all the other body processes that take place daily. It also lubricates our joints and cartilages resulting in fluid movement. When dehydrated, the body rations water away from the joints, which means greater friction and joint, knee, and back pain which leads to injuries and arthritis. Water helps our bodies remove toxins in many different ways like it flushes toxins and waste from the body through urination and perspiration, it also helps in reducing constipation and aids in bowel movements, which ensures that waste removal is done quickly and regularly before it becomes poisonous. This waste build-up can occur in the body if dehydration becomes a regular occurrence and this can cause headaches, toxicity, and illness.

Water therapy or hydrotherapy is treating with any form of water. Hot water, cold water, steam or water imbued with the therapeutic goodness of herbs, spices, fruits, and even condiments. While detoxifying or fasting it is very essential to drink more water so that the body can be cleansed of all the toxins that have accumulated.

THERAPEUTIC WATER: THE DIY KIT

Making your own therapeutic water at home is very easy. Just remember to use a clean glass bottle and if you are going to be travelling with it, please put the bottle in a jute or cloth bag… your wine bottle bags will come to good use now!

All you need to do is go through the chart below to identify your health condition and to zero in on the ingredients you will need. Then simply add the ingredients to a litre of water, and let them soak in the water for an hour before starting to drink the water.

My advice would be to make just one litre of the therapeutic water. Drink from mid-morning till 7 pm. Keep adding fresh water to the bottle as it comes to an end. This way you will also be able to keep a tab on how much water you have had throughout the day. You can refer to the following table to make your own therapeutic water:

Ailment/Disease	What to add per 1 litre of water
To increase energy	5 star anise
To decrease blood pressure	2 stalks of fresh celery + 5 parsley leaves
To decrease edema	Juice of 1 lemon + 1 tsp dried celery
To increase metabolic rate	2 star anise + a 2 inch quill of cinnamon
To cleanse the system	1 lemon cut into 4 bits
To detoxify the liver	5 basil leaves + 10 mint leaves
To decrease blood sugars	10 methi seeds + 1 tsp cinnamon powder
To increase immunity	1 bay leaf + 5 green cardamoms
To prevent colds	2 cloves + 3 green cardamoms
For glowing skin	2 thin slices of an orange + 5 mulled strawberries
For headaches	1 inch piece of ginger + 4-5 slices of apple

Contd...

Ailment/Disease	What to add per 1 litre of water
For gas/indigestion	1 tsp roasted ajwain + 2 peppercorns
For halitosis	1 tsp chopped lemon grass + 10 mint leaves
For anxiety	5 strands of kesar (saffron)
For depression	10 rose petals + 2 strands kesar
For lethargy	½ lemon + 4–5 strawberries + 2 star anise
For muscle cramps	½ thinly sliced orange +10 basil leaves
For nausea	1 tsp coriander seeds + 5 sage leaves
For hyperacidity	1 thinly sliced apple + 1 tsp ginger juice
For stomach cramps	¼ tsp nutmeg powder + 2 roasted bay leaves
For menstrual cramps	1 inch piece of ginger + 1 tsp fennel
For skin allergies	2 pieces of kokum with a tsp rock sugar + a pinch of salt
For a hangover	1 tsp chopped ginger + ½ apple or pear
For mouth ulcers	1 sprig of fresh coriander + 4 tbsp melon cubes
For fevers	juice of 1 onion + 1 tbsp honey

It's surprisingly simple but it works! Drinking therapeutic water daily is like the rich chocolate icing on a super yummy cake. It will not only help in you be in good health, but also remind you of drinking water daily! Remember, without good health, all your work will go down the drain.

Don't forget to store your therapeutic water in a clean glass bottle and carry it along everywhere you go.

5

Oils that Cure

IF YOU WOULD LIKE TO GIVE A ZING TO THE FOOD YOU ARE cooking on a daily basis why not try spicing up the oils that you use? Not only will this enhance the flavour of the food but it will also provide a host of therapeutic benefits, thereby keeping your loved ones in the pink of health.

If you are making this at home please ensure that the bottles are clean. Wash the bottles well and rinse with a good sterilizing solution. I prefer to use the sterilizing solution sold at the local chemist for sterilizing baby-feeding bottles. If you can find cork stoppers for the bottles, then please buy and use them. The aromatic flavour of the oil is always better in a bottle that has a cork stopper. Once the spiced oil is ready you can strain it and transfer it into another clean bottle, although I prefer not to strain it. That way the flavour of the oil gets stronger after sometime and adds yet another dimension to your cooking.

If, however, it gets too strong for your liking you can always make it mild by adding more oil.

Use the aromatic oils for pickling or for Indian, Mediterranean, Chinese, or continental cooking, or even as a salad dressing. They add a totally different dimension to your marinades, gravies, salad dressings, sauces, etc.

SPICY GARLIC OIL

In the winter months, most people are prone to upper respiratory tract infections due to the higher amount of pollutant particulate matter in the air. Spicy garlic oil helps in the prevention of colds and is beneficial to the entire family.

Ingredients

5 red chillies
10 black peppercorns
1 litre virgin olive oil
5 bay leaves
4 cloves of ginger and garlic

Preparation

❖ Fill a 1-litre clean bottle with virgin olive oil up to 2 inches below the rim.
❖ Add 5 red chillies, 10 black peppercorns, 5 roasted bay leaves, and 4 peeled and halved cloves of garlic.

❖ Cover and store for 2–3 weeks or until the flavour is well pronounced.

❖ Use for lamb, chicken, and lentil gravies.

STAR ANISE, ONION, AND GINGER OIL

You must have noticed how your energy levels dip in the rainy season. Instead of rushing off to work in the morning during a heavy downpour, all you want to do is curl up and sleep some more. In this case, star anise, onion, and ginger oil are particularly helpful to give you an energy boost. This is perfect for those grey monsoon months.

Ingredients

1 litre sesame oil
3 star anise
1 onion
20 gm ginger

Preparation

❖ Fill a 1-litre clean bottle with sesame oil up to 2 inches below the rim.

❖ Add 2 inches of cleaned, peeled and lightly crushed ginger, 3 star anise, and 1 small peeled and diced onion.

❖ Cover and leave aside for 2–3 weeks or until the flavour is well pronounced.

❖ Use to cook Chinese dishes especially seafood and chicken. It can also be used to cook tofu, paneer, and soyabeans.

CELERY, CLOVE, AND LEMON GRASS OIL

All those who need to keep their high blood pressure in check will benefit from this oil.

Ingredients

1 litre groundnut oil
2 stalks fresh celery
3 cloves
2 stalks lemon grass

Preparation

❖ Fill a 1-litre clean bottle with groundnut oil up to 2 inches below the rim.
❖ Add 2 stalks of fresh celery (after discarding the root and the leaves), 3 cloves, and 2 stalks of lemon grass (after discarding the root).
❖ Cover and leave aside for 2–3 weeks or until the flavour is well pronounced.
❖ Use this oil when cooking vegetables, daals, and fish.

ORANGE, WALNUT, AND CINNAMON OIL

This oil acts as an antioxidant and a detoxifier.

Ingredients

1 litre sunflower oil
2 crushed walnut halves
2-inch quill of cinnamon
Orange rind

Preparation

❖ Fill a 1-litre clean bottle with sunflower oil up to 2 inches below the rim.
❖ Add 2 walnut halves that have been slightly crushed, a 2-inch quill of cinnamon, and a couple of pieced of cleaned orange rind.
❖ Cover and leave aside for 2–3 weeks or until the flavour is well pronounced.
❖ Use this oil to make salad dressings, mayonnaise, and also as a marinade for chicken, fish, and paneer.

CARDAMOM AND FENNEL SEED OIL

When you're feeling blue, depressed, hurt, or anxious all you need to do is to start cooking in cardamom and fennel seed oil. Happy days are here again!

Ingredients

1 litre rice bran/groundnut oil
5 green cardamoms
1 tbsp roasted fennel seeds

Preparation

❖ Fill a 1-litre clean bottle with rice bran or groundnut oil up to 2 inches below the rim.
❖ Add 5 green cardamoms and a tablespoon of roasted fennel seeds.
❖ Cover and leave aside for 2–3 weeks or until the flavour is well pronounced.
❖ This oil is best used for Indian gravies.

SPICED VINEGARS

Vinegar is an essential ingredient in most kitchens. From cooking and cleaning, to gardening and home remedies, vinegar is one of the most versatile—and economical—products you can have on hand. Enjoying a salad with a tangy vinaigrette dressing is one of the most popular ways to use vinegar in the kitchen.

But that's just the beginning! Regular and flavoured vinegars are versatile recipe ingredients that don't only add flavour and distinction, but can also contribute to good health! Spiced and flavoured vinegars add another dimension in the preparation of sauces, marinades, gravies, salad dressings, and mayonnaise. Apple cider vinegar, balsamic vinegar, red wine vinegar, and white wine vinegar are best suited for making spiced vinegars.

Here are the recipes of a few very special vinegars with great health benefits.

GARLIC AND PARSLEY VINEGAR

This vinegar is extremely effective in reducing blood pressure and is great for adding flavour to food.

Ingredients

10 cloves of garlic
1 tbsp dried parsley
1000 ml vinegar

Preparation

❖ Crush 10 cloves of garlic and 1 tbsp dried parsley.
❖ Heat 500 ml vinegar and pour over the garlic and parsley.
❖ Let it cool and then add another 500 ml of cold vinegar.

- ❖ Cover and keep aside for 2 weeks.
- ❖ For a milder flavour strain and use, else use as it is.

CHILLI GINGER VINEGAR

This spiced vinegar is great to improve immunity and increase metabolic rate of the body.

Ingredients

50 gm peeled ginger
4 Kashmiri chillies
1000 ml vinegar

Preparation

- ❖ Crush the ginger and chillies.
- ❖ Heat 500 ml vinegar and pour over the ginger and chillies.
- ❖ Let it cool and then add another 500 ml of cold vinegar.
- ❖ Cover and keep aside for 2 weeks.
- ❖ For a milder flavour strain and use, else use as it is.

CARDAMOM AND SAFFRON VINEGAR

Use this spiced vinegar to reduce anxiety and depression. It also enhances the flavour in Indian gravies and curries.

Ingredients

- ❖ 20 green cardamoms
- ❖ 20 strands of kesar
- ❖ 1000 ml vinegar

Preparation

- ❖ Crush the cardamoms and kesar.
- ❖ Heat 500 ml vinegar and pour over the cardamoms and kesar.
- ❖ Let it cool and then add another 500 ml of cold vinegar.
- ❖ Cover and keep aside for 2 weeks.
- ❖ For a milder flavour strain and use, else use as it is.

SAUNF AND DILL VINEGAR

This spiced vinegar serves as a good digestive, and has a lovely flavour to it due to the blend of saunf and dill.

Ingredients

1 tbsp roasted saunf
1 tbsp roasted dill seeds (suva)
1000 ml vinegar

Preparation

❖ Mix the roasted saunf and dill seeds.
❖ Heat 500 ml vinegar and pour over this mix.
❖ Let it cool and then add another 500 ml of cold vinegar.
❖ Cover and keep aside for 2 weeks.
❖ For a milder flavour strain and use, else use as is.

GREEN ONION VINEGAR

Another flavourful vinegar, this one is used to improve immunity and decrease mucus, especially in cases of a cold.

Ingredients

5 bulbs of spring onions, quartered
1000 ml vinegar

Preparation

❖ Crush the green onion bulbs.
❖ Heat 500 ml vinegar and pour over the crushed green onions.

❖ Let it cool and then add another 500 ml of cold vinegar.
❖ Cover and keep aside for 2 weeks.
❖ For a milder flavour strain and use, else use as is.

The kitchen is a place for not just cooking, but healing. Using spiced oils and vinegars made by you in your kitchen will go a long way in keeping your family and you both healthy and happy. Especially as these are also really tasty. Why have medicine when you have the magic touch . . . that too in a natural form in the comfort of your own home.

PART 2

USING HERBS TO PREVENT AND CURE MINOR ILLNESSES

6

Prevention and Cure of Common Illnesses

COMMON ILLNESSES ARE LIKE THOSE EVERYDAY THINGS FOR which there is no practical solution which the doctor can give. The only thing we end up doing is taking medicines, and then some more medicines, which means that we're constantly abusing our bodies. However, we know how harsh the effects of these common illnesses can be, rendering us incapable to go to work or function to the best of our abilities. There is a ray of light in this bleak scenario: naturopathy. The correct combination of herbs and spices along with the right diet can do wonders to treat these illnesses.

I once had a patient, Vaibhavi, who had Googled every diet possible on the Internet. She lost weight each time, but was extremely unhappy with the consequences. Her health suffered primarily because most of her online regimens did not take into account her hectic lifestyle. She was a banker with a leading foreign bank who worked hard, and partied harder. Being constricted to only a limited spectrum of food, her food consumption was very low, as a result of which her immune system was compromised. She always had a cold or an allergy or a headache, and resorted to taking allopathic medicine. This further worsened her health. **The spice mix I asked her to prepare consisted of cinnamon, cumin, fennel, mint, cardamom, star anise, coriander, mango powder, and poppy seeds.** She started taking this thrice a day, and within three months she had lost the desired amount of weight, without it affecting her health or her missing even a single day of work or night of partying. So, you see, common illnesses are not that hard to treat.

Here I discuss some of the most common problems that we suffer from and their remedies.

COMMON COLD

The common cold is the most frequently occurring illness in the world, and it is a leading cause of doctor visits and missed days from school and work. There is no cure for the common cold, and antibiotics play no role in treatment. **Antibiotics are effective only against illnesses caused by bacteria, and colds are caused by viruses.** Because some two hundred different viruses can cause a cold, the body never builds up resistance against all of them. In addition, new cold virus strains are constantly developing. For these reasons, colds are a frequent and recurring problem.

How is the common cold transmitted?

The most common ways a cold spreads is either by direct contact with infected secretions from surfaces or by inhaling the airborne virus after people sneeze or cough. If you come in contact when someone who has a cold, you are more likely to catch their infection. A fact to remember is that cold viruses live on our day-to-day objects like coffee cups, pens, computer keyboards, telephones and books for many hours, and hence you can get a cold from contact with these things.

How long does it last?

The common cold generally lasts anywhere between four days to a fortnight, and most people show significant recovery in a week. There's a saying: it takes seven days for a common cold to cure on its own and one week with the help of medicines. So technically there's not much you can do!

What are the symptoms and signs of the common cold?

The symptoms of the common cold typically begin two to three days after acquiring the infection.

The symptoms of a common cold often vary but some of the most common symptoms are:

❖ headache
❖ watery eyes
❖ sore throat

- ❖ fever
- ❖ body aches
- ❖ sneezing
- ❖ coughing
- ❖ nasal stuffiness
- ❖ exhaustion
- ❖ congestions of the chest

Does it have anything to do with exposure to cold weather?

Though the common cold usually occurs in the fall and winter months, the cold weather itself does not cause the common cold. Rather, it is thought that during cold weather months, people spend more time indoors in close proximity to each other, thus facilitating the spread of the virus. For this same reason, school going children are particularly prone to acquiring the common cold.

A well balanced diet helps your body function optimally. Nutrient rich foods not only help to fight infections they also protect you from illnesses. A common mistake made by people is to rely only on dietary supplements like vitamins and minerals for their nutrition, not realizing that this limits their diet to only known nutritional compounds and fails to give them the full benefits of other nutrients which are present in our food that are extremely essential for our bodies.

Let's look at some of the top recommendations for staying healthy:

Eating foods high in antioxidants

Beta-carotene and Vitamins C and E may be a good way to help build a strong immune system. Antioxidants are essential nutrients. They help protect your body against life's stressors and are thought to play a role in the body's cell protection system. Including more raw fruits and vegetables in your diet is the best way to ensure a high intake of antioxidants. And when you cook these super-nutrients, be sure you cook them using as little liquid as possible to prevent nutrient loss.

Consuming foods high in bioflavonoids

Such foods may also help you stay healthy. These biochemically active substances accompany Vitamin C in plants and act as an antioxidant. You can find bioflavonoids in the pulp and white core that runs through the centre of citrus fruits, green peppers, lemons, limes, oranges, cherries, and grapes.

Strengthening the immune system

You can do this by introducing glutathione in your diet. Glutathione is another nutrient that has been found to strengthen the immune system so it can fight infections. **This powerful antioxidant is most plentiful in the red, pulpy area of the watermelon near the rind.** It can also be found in broccoli, Brussels sprouts, cabbage, cauliflower, spinach, and other cruciferous vegetables.

Eating foods high in phytochemicals

Such foods are also important for wellness. Foods rich in phytochemicals include apples, apricots, broccoli, Brussels sprouts, cabbage, carrots, cauliflower, garlic, legumes, onions, red peppers, soybeans, sweet potatoes, and tomatoes.

Supplementation with Vitamin C helps prevent susceptibility to colds and viral infections. It is important to start the

REMEDIES TO CURE/PREVENT COLDS

❖ Dilute 2 tbsp lime juice, a pinch of paprika and 1 tsp of honey in half a cup water and have it every morning to prevent colds. Have this concoction thrice a day if you already have a cold.

❖ Another good remedy to treat a cold as well as a dry cough is to make a brew of 2 tbsp of ginger juice, 1 tbsp garlic juice a pinch of haldi powder and 2 green elaichi in 100 ml water. Bring to a boil and allow it to simmer for 2 minutes. Strain, add 1 tsp rock sugar (mishri) and drink warm. Repeat two to three times a day until the cough and cold subsides.

❖ Boil 5 green elaichi and 2 cloves in 2 litres of water and drink this water daily to improve immunity.

Remember, treating a common cold is more about improving immunity than anything else. So improve your diet, and stay healthy.

supplementation much ahead of the winter season. Ideally, you should start increasing the amounts of Vitamin C in the diet around the time of Dussehra and continue until Holi. 200 mg of Vitamin C is sufficient per day. If you already have a cold then you should consume a minimum of 500 mg.

FEVER

Fever happens when there is an increase in body temperature. Anything above the normal body temperature (98.6°F). However, fever is not medically significant till the body temperature is above 100.4°F. Any temperature which is more than normal but below 100.4°F (38°C) is known as a low-grade fever. The primary reason why low-grade fevers should go untreated, until of course they are accompanied by other troubling symptoms, is because fever acts as one of the body's best defenses against the bacteria and viruses which die at higher temperatures.

Fevers of 104°F or higher demand immediate home treatment and subsequent medical attention, as they can result in delirium and convulsions, particularly in infants and children.

What causes a fever?

Fever is the result of an immune response by your body to a foreign invader. These foreign invaders include viruses, bacteria, fungi, drugs, or other toxins.

These foreign invaders are considered fever-producing substances (called pyrogens), which trigger the body's immune response. Pyrogens tell the hypothalamus to increase the temperature set point in order to help the body fight off the infection.

Fever is a common symptom of most infections. In children, immunizations or teething may cause low-grade fever. Autoimmune disorders, medication reactions, seizures, may also cause fevers.

What are the signs and symptoms of a fever?

A fever can make you feel very uncomfortable. Signs and symptoms of a fever include the following:

❖ temperature greater than 100.4°F (38°C) in adults and children
❖ shivering, shaking, chills
❖ aching muscles and joints
❖ headaches
❖ intermittent sweat
❖ rapid heart rate or palpitations
❖ skin flushing
❖ feeling faint, dizzy, or lightheaded
❖ weakness
❖ with very high temperature (> 104°F/40°C), convulsions, hallucination, or confusion are possible

REMEDIES TO CURE A FEVER

❖ Dill seeds (suva) help during febrile conditions. Roast 1 tbsp suva seeds along with 2 peppercorns and 1 tsp kalonji. Boil this in 150 ml water for 3 to 4 minutes. Allow to steep for 10 minutes. Then strain, add a pinch of cinnamon powder and drink warm. Repeat whenever the body temperature crosses 100 degrees.

❖ Another good remedy for bringing down fever is tulsi leaves. Boil 20 leaves with 2 cloves in 1 litre water until it reduces to half a litre. Drink this every 2 hours.

When a young child has fever never allow the body temperature to cross 100 degrees. If it goes above 100, then immediately give the child a tepid water sponge and wrap the child in a woollen blanket until the fever breaks. Continue giving the dill seed decoction. Add honey if the child fusses about drinking it.

Also, don't forget that fever is a sign of the body fighting; hence there must be some underlying reason for it. Reducing the temperature is important, but finding the reason behind is imperative.

HEADACHE

Headaches have numerous causes and so many people suffer from headaches, making treatment difficult on occasion. There are three major categories of headaches:

❖ primary headaches
❖ secondary headaches
❖ cranial neuralgias, facial pain, and other headaches

What are primary headaches?

Primary headaches include migraine, tension, and cluster headaches, as well as a variety of other less common types of headache.

Tension headaches are the most common type of primary headache. Up to 90 percent of adults have had or will have tension headaches. Tension headaches occur more commonly among women than men.

Migraine headaches are the second most common type of primary headache. Migraine headaches affect children as well as adults. Before puberty, boys and girls are affected equally by migraine headaches, but after puberty, more women than men are affected.

Cluster headaches are a rare type of primary headache affecting 0.1 percent of the population. It more commonly affects men in their late twenties though women and children can also suffer these types of headache.

Primary headaches can affect the quality of life. Some people have occasional headaches that resolve quickly while others are debilitated. While these headaches are not life-threatening, they may be associated with symptoms that can mimic strokes or intra-cerebral bleeding.

What are secondary headaches?

Secondary headaches are caused due to an underlying structural problem in the head or neck. There are numerous causes of this type of headache, ranging from bleeding in the brain, a tumour, meningitis, or encephalitis.

What are cranial neuralgias, facial pain, and other headaches?

Neuralgia means nerve pain (neur= nerve + algia=pain). Cranial neuralgia describes a group of headaches that occur because the nerves in the head and upper neck become inflamed and become the source of the pain in the head. Facial pain and a variety of other causes for headache are included in this category.

What are the symptoms of tension headaches?

These are the most common types of headaches and there causes are not known. Emotional stress, physical stress, or working at a desk all day might cause one. The pain symptoms of a tension headache are:
❖ pain begins in the back of the head and upper neck and is described as a band-like tightness or pressure;

- often described as pressure encircling the head with the most intense pressure over the eyebrows;
- pain is usually mild (not disabling) and affecting both sides of the head;
- the pain occurs sporadically but can occur frequently and even daily in some people; and
- the pain allows most people to function normally, despite the headache.

REMEDIES FOR HEADACHES

The first step towards treating or remedying a headache is to identify the cause of it. After that there are simple enough tricks that will ease your pain, without the help of painkillers!

If it is due to eye strain:

- Simple eye exercises like blinking, moving the eyes from side to side, and rotating the head in the clockwise and anti-clockwise direction helps.

- Rest for 10 minutes with an eye pack made by dipping flat cotton disks in cold water; for greater relief, you can add a few drops of rose water. If this is not possible then simply cup your eyes in the palm of your hands and blink rapidly, your headache will vanish.

If it is due to starvation/low blood sugar/iron deficiency:

❖ Eat 5 black raisins with a tsp of white sesame seeds before you eat anything else. Chew this well and you will get quick relief.

If it is a hangover:

❖ Drink tomato and celery juice—and a promise to self never to binge drink again!

If it is due to an increase in your BP:

❖ Drink a cup of green tea along with a fig or prune.

❖ Immerse your legs for 20 minutes in a bucket of warm water with 2 tbsp salt. Rotate your ankles in the water to improve circulation. Your BP will decrease and your headache will be history.

JET LAG

Jet lag, also called desynchronosis and flight fatigue, is a temporary disorder that causes fatigue, insomnia, and other symptoms as a result of air travel across time zones. It is considered a circadian rhythm sleep disorder, which is a disruption of the internal body clock.

What are other symptoms and signs of jet lag?

Besides fatigue and insomania, a jet-lag sufferer may experience a number of physical and emotional symtoms including anxiety, constipation, diarrhoea, dehydration, headache, irritability, nausea, sweating, coordination problems, dizziness, and even memory loss. Some individuals report additional symptoms, such as heartbeat irregularities and increased susceptibility to illness. An important thing to note about jet lag is that children also suffer the same symptoms as adults.

Why does jet lag occur?

Jet lag occurs because the body of the traveler takes time to adjust immediately to the time in a different zone. So if you're travelling abroad, say to London, your body continues to function on Indian time. While the body tries to cope with this new change, things like exhaustion, temporary insomnia, irritability and an inability to concentrate might set in. Apart from this, you might get constipation or diarrhoea because of the changed schedule.

What is the role of melatonin in jet lag?

Melatonin is a hormone that plays a key role in body rhythms and jet lag. After the sun sets, the eyes perceive darkness and alert the hypothalamus to begin releasing melatonin, which promotes sleep. Conversely, when the eyes perceive sunlight, they tell the hypothalamus to withhold melatonin production.

However, the hypothalamus cannot readjust its schedule instantly; it takes several days.

How long does jet lag last?

Recovering from jet lag depends on the number of time zones crossed while travelling. In general, the body will adjust to the new time zone at the rate of one or two time zones per day. For example, if you crossed six time zones, the body will typically adjust to this time change in three to five days.

How to cope with jet lag?

There are various home remedies that aid in the prevention of jet lag and help in fast recovery of the symptoms. Here are a few tips that will help you avoid and/or minimize the effects of jet lag:

❖ **Exercise**: A healthy and fit body will automatically ensure that you can better cope with the trying conditions of air travel. Get enough rest and exercise before you're heading for a long journey. Your physical stamina and conditioning will allow you to deal with jet lag better after you land.

❖ **Get medical advice**: If you are patient with a medical condition that needs special monitoring, you need to check with your doctor well in advance of your departure.

❖ **Change your schedule**: If you will be staying in the new time zone for more than just a few days, you need to adjust your body to it before you leave. For example, if you are travelling from India to the US, you should set your daily routine back by around two hours three to four weeks before you leave. The next week, set it back by another hour, and so on and so forth. By doing this, you will save your body the shock of jet lag and a new time schedule immediately.

❖ **Avoid alcohol**: Refrain from drinking alcoholic beverages one day before, during and after your flight as it can cause dehydration, nausea and spoil your sleeping schedule.

❖ **Avoid caffeine**: Avoid caffeinated drinks before, during and after the flight as it can also cause dehydration and spoil your sleep cycle.

❖ **Drink water**: Airplanes are air conditioned and being in one for too long can cause dehydration.

❖ **Stretch your legs**: While seated during your flight, exercise your legs from time to time. Go, take a walk down the aisle. Every hour or two, get up and walk around. Do not take sleeping pills, and do not nap for more than an hour at a time.

❖ **Adapt to the local schedule**: The sooner you adapt to the local schedule, the quicker your body will adjust. Therefore, if you arrive at noon local time (but 6 am your time), eat lunch, not breakfast. During the day, expose your body to sunlight by taking walks or sitting in outdoor cafés. The sunlight will cue your hypothalamus to reduce the production of sleep-inducing melatonin during the day, thereby initiating the process of resetting your internal clock.

IN A NUTSHELL

Just remember and follow these things, and you should be fine and jet-lag free!

❖ Three days before you travel eat high protein breakfasts and lunches and for dinner have a carbohydrate-rich meal.

❖ A day before your flight (or the day of the flight if the flight is late at night), have very light meals like fruits, salads, and soups.

❖ Drink plenty of water on the flight to keep yourself hydrated. Avoid caffeine as much as possible.

❖ Once you land have a hearty high-protein meal and continue drinking at least four more glasses of water than your usual allowance.

❖ After dinner have 1 tsp nutmeg powder dissolved in a cup of warm milk. You will definitely sleep for a minimum of five hours and wake up feeling refreshed.

INSOMNIA

Insomnia is a disorder that can make it hard to fall asleep, hard to stay asleep, or both. With insomnia, you usually awaken not feeling refreshed, which takes a toll on your ability to function during the day. Insomnia can sap not only your energy level and mood but also your health, work performance, and quality of life.

How much sleep is enough varies from person to person. Most adults need seven to eight hours a night. Many adults experience insomnia at some point, but some people have long-term (chronic) insomnia.

You don't have to put up with sleepless nights. Simple changes in your daily habits can help.

What are the causes of insomnia?

* **Stress**: A very common cause, worrying about work, health and family keeps your mind alert at night, causing insomnia. Also, certain stressful events also make sleep difficult.
* **Anxiety**: Daily anxieties both cause difficulty in sleeping.
* **Depression**: If you're depressed, the chemical imbalances in your brain and the various problems that accompany depression stop you from relaxing and hence you either sleep too much or too little.
* **Medication**: Many over-the-counter medications like painkillers, decongestants, etc., contain caffeine and other stimulants making sleeping harder. Apart from this, prescription drugs like antidepressants, heart and BP medications, allergy medications, stimulants and corticosteroids also interfere with sleep.
* **Caffeine, nicotine, and alcohol**: Coffee, tea, cola, and other caffeine-containing drinks are stimulants. Drinking

coffee in the late afternoon and later can keep you from falling asleep at night. Nicotine in tobacco products is another stimulant and can cause insomnia. Keep in mind that alcohol may help you sleep, but it stops the deeper stages of sleep and often makes you wake up in the middle of the night.

❖ **Medical conditions**: If you have chronic pain, breathing difficulties, or a need to urinate frequently, you might develop insomnia. Conditions linked with insomnia include arthritis, cancer, heart failure, lung disease, gastroesophageal reflux disease (GERD), overactive thyroid, stroke, Parkinson's disease, and Alzheimer's disease. Making sure that your medical conditions are well treated may help with your insomnia. If you have arthritis, for example, taking a pain reliever before bed may help you sleep better.

❖ **Change in your environment or work schedule**: Constant travel or working a late or early shift can disrupt your body's circadian rhythms, making it difficult to sleep. Your circadian rhythms act as internal clocks, guiding such things as your sleep-wake cycle, metabolism, and body temperature.

❖ **Poor sleep habits**: Habits that help promote good sleep are called sleep hygiene. Poor sleep hygiene includes an irregular sleep schedule, stimulating activities before bed, an uncomfortable sleep environment, and use of your bed for activities other than sleep or sex.

❖ **'Learned' insomnia**: This may occur when you worry excessively about not being able to sleep well and try too hard to fall asleep. Most people with this condition sleep better when they're away from their usual sleep environment or when they don't try to sleep, such as when they're watching TV or reading.

❖ **Eating too much late in the evening**: Having a light snack before bedtime is okay, but eating too much may cause you to feel physically uncomfortable while lying down, making it difficult to get to sleep. Many people also experience heartburn, a backflow of acid and food from the stomach into the oesophagus after eating. This uncomfortable feeling may keep you awake.

Good sleep habits for beating insomnia

To beat insomnia, you need proper sleep hygiene or good sleep habits. Follow these tips and see the results for yourself.

❖ **Fresh sheets, linen, and a sturdy mattress**: Simple point but it can make all the difference. There's nothing like sleeping on a firm but inviting mattress.

❖ **Sleeping schedule**: Ensure that you go to sleep and wake up at the same time every day. Also try to avoid taking naps during the day as they make you less sleepy in the night. If you feel that you just need to sleep in the afternoon, try a cat nap instead; it can immediately recharge you.

❖ **Coffee and alcohol**: You already know this but both coffee and alcohol inhibit sleep because they are stimulants.

❖ **Exercise**: A suggestion from experts includes not exercising three to four hours before you go to sleep. This is because if you exercise close to bedtime, it stimulates you, making it harder to fall asleep. At the same time, remember to get regular exercise.

❖ **Eat light before sleeping**: Remember to eat a light snack before you sleep, as it helps in sleeping. However, avoid eating a heavy meal late in the day.

❖ **Turn off the lights**: Your body has its own clock. If you turn out the lights, your body will understand that it's night and prepare to shut down.

If you can't fall asleep and don't feel drowsy, get up and read, or do something that is not overly stimulating until you feel sleepy.

If you find yourself lying awake worrying about things, try making a to-do list before you go to bed. This may help you to not focus on those worries overnight.

REMEDIES FOR A GOOD NIGHT'S SLEEP

Soak 2 tsp khus khus, 5 black raisins, 5 strands of kesar along with a pinch of grated nutmeg in 4 tbsp of milk for two hours every evening.

If you want to fall asleep two hours after eating dinner then you should have this combination prior to dinner.

If, however, you are going to out after dinner and will be up till late, then have the khus khus combination after dinner or once you reach home.

Do this daily for a week or two, and after that, have this concoction whenever you feel stressed out and realize you won't be able to sleep. I can guarantee you'll feel much better in the morning.

MENSTRUAL CRAMPS

Menstrual cramps are pains in the belly and pelvic areas that are experienced by a woman as a result of her menstrual period. Menstrual cramps are often mistaken for premenstrual syndrome (PMS) because the symptoms of both disorders can often be experienced as a continual process. Many women often experience both PMS and menstrual cramps.

What is dysmenorrhoea?

Medically, menstrual cramps is known as dysmenorrhoea. Dysmenorrhoea is of two types: primary and secondary.

There is no underlying gynaecological condition which causes the pain in primary dysmenorrhoea. This may begin between six months to a year after menarche (the starting of menstruation).

Why are some cramps so painful?

Menstrual cramps are caused by uterine contractions. The cramping sensation is intensified when clots or pieces of bloody tissue from the lining of the uterus pass through the cervix, especially if a woman's cervical canal is narrow.

The difference between menstrual cramps that are more painful and those that are less painful may be related to a woman's prostaglandin levels. Women with menstrual cramps have elevated levels of prostaglandins in the endometrium (uterine lining) when compared with women who do not experience cramps. These cramps are extremely similar to what a pregnant woman goes through when she is given the medicine prostaglandin to induce labour.

What are the symptoms of menstrual cramps?

Menstrual cramps begin in the lower abdomen and pelvis. The discomfort can extend to the lower back or legs. The cramps can be a quite painful or simply a dull ache. They can be periodic or continual.

Menstrual cramps usually start shortly before the menstrual period, peak within twenty-four hours after the onset of the bleeding, and subside again after a day or two.

They may be accompanied by a headache and/or nausea, which can lead, although infrequently, to the point of vomiting. Menstrual cramps can also be accompanied by either constipation or diarrhoea because the prostaglandins, which cause smooth muscles to contract, are found in both the uterus and intestinal tract. Some women experience an urge to urinate more frequently.

REMEDY FOR MENSTRUAL CRAMPS

If you generally suffer from period cramps try this remedy a week before your period.

❖ Dry roast 4 tbsp of coriander seeds along with 10 peppercorns, 1 tbsp of ginger powder, 1 tbsp of white sesame seeds and 3 tbsp of fennel (saunf).

❖ Powder this and store in an airtight container.

❖ Have 1 tsp thrice a day along with a small piece of mishri (rock sugar). Continue having this until the second day of your period.

VARICOSE VEINS

Varicose veins are dark blue, twisted, enlarged veins near the surface of the skin. In normal veins, valves in the vein keep blood moving forward towards the heart. With varicose veins, the valves do not function properly, causing blood to stay in the vein. Blood that pools causes the vein to swell. They are most common in the legs and ankles, although it may occur in other parts of the body. They usually aren't serious, but they can sometimes lead to other problems.

What are the causes?

❖ defective valves from birth (congenitally defective valves)
❖ pregnancy
❖ thrombophlebitis
❖ standing for a long time and having increased pressure in the abdomen.

Some people do not have any symptoms. Mild symptoms may include:
❖ heaviness, burning, aching, tiredness, or pain in your legs. Symptoms may be worse after you stand or sit for long periods of time
❖ swelling in the feet and ankles
❖ itching over the vein

More serious symptoms include:
❖ leg swelling
❖ swelling and calf pain after you sit or stand for long periods of time

Skin changes, such as:
❖ colour changes
❖ dry, thinned skin
❖ inflammation
❖ scaling
❖ open sores, or bleeding after a minor injury

How to prevent varicose veins?

Varicose veins can be prevented by following the following remedies:

* ❖ Eat sulphur-rich food like onions, garlic, eggs and asparagus, which reduce the tendency of blood to clot.
* ❖ Zinc-rich food like shellfish, wholegrains, pumpkin seeds, sunflower seeds, melon seeds, and cucumber seeds help in wound healing.
* ❖ Vitamin C and flavonoids found in berries, kiwis, and citrus fruits help to strengthen the walls of the blood vessels.

REMEDIES FOR VARICOSE VEINS

* ❖ Make a mix of cumin seeds, cardamom powder, kasoori methi, onion seeds, fennel, and coriander powder. Take a tsp of this on rising and at bedtime.

* ❖ Drink plenty of water. Add a couple of slices of lemon, orange, and a few berries to the water.

GOUT

This is an extremely common disease. Gout is a kind of arthritis that occurs when uric acid builds up in blood and causes joint inflammation. Acute gout is a painful condition that typically affects one joint, while chronic gout is repeated episodes of pain and inflammation, which may involve more than one joint.

What causes Gout?

The exact cause of gout is unknown. Gout may run in families. It is more common in men, in women after menopause, and those who drink alcohol. People who take certain medicines, such as hydrochlorothiazide and other water pills, may have higher levels of uric acid in the blood. This condition is more likely to occur after taking medicines that interfere with the removal of uric acid from the body.

Gout is caused by having higher-than-normal levels of uric acid in your body. This may occur if:
❖ your body makes too much uric acid
❖ your body has a hard time getting rid of uric acid
❖ if too much uric acid builds up in the fluid around the joints (synovial fluid), uric acid crystals form. These crystals cause the joint to swell up and become inflamed.

The condition may also develop in people with:
❖ diabetes
❖ kidney disease
❖ obesity
❖ sickle cell anaemia and other types of anaemia
❖ leukaemia and other blood cancers

What are the symptoms of acute gout?

Symptoms usually involve only one or a few joints. The big toe, knee, or ankle joints are most often affected. The pain starts suddenly, often during the night and is often throbbing. The joint appears warm and red. It is usually very tender (it hurts to lay even a thin cloth over it). And there may be a fever.

The attack may go away in a few days, but may return from time to time. Additional attacks often last longer. After a first gout attack, people will have no symptoms. Half of patients have another attack before they realize that something is not right.

Some people may develop chronic gout. Those with chronic arthritis develop joint damage and loss of motion in the joints. They will have joint pain and other symptoms most of the time.

Alcohol intake, especially beer, has been linked to gout attacks. Avoid fasting and rapid weight loss programmes as they might bring on a gout attack. To flush out uric acid, drink plenty of fluids.

How can gout be prevented?

❖ Eat foods rich in folic acid, like cabbage, spinach, methi, mint, coriander, etc. which help to control the levels of uric acid in the blood.

❖ Vitamin C-rich foods like grapefruit, celery, pineapple, cherries, and citrus fruits help to flush out uric acid from the blood via the urine.

❖ Avoid liver, kidney, red meat, fish, shellfish, oats, yeast, mushrooms, vinegar, and alcohol.

REMEDIES FOR GOUT

❖ Make a mix of dried mint powder, cumin powder, flax meal, dried parsley, fennel, and turmeric powder. Have 2 tsp of this mix after lunch and 1 tsp after dinner.

❖ Drink 2 litres of water infused with 15 mint leaves and 10 basil leaves.

IMMUNITY

What is the function of the immune system?

Don't you get jealous of those people who never seem to fall sick? It's because of their immune system; it works overtime! The immune system helps protect the body from harmful substances called antigens. Examples of antigens include bacteria, viruses, toxins, cancer cells, and foreign blood or tissues from another person or species. We often tell those people who fall sick very frequently that their immune system is weak, or compromised. Doctors might actually get you tested for your antigen level.

When the immune system detects an antigen, it responds by

producing proteins called antibodies that destroy the harmful substances. The immune system response also involves a process called phagocytosis. During this process, certain white blood cells swallow and destroy bacteria and other foreign substances. Proteins called 'complements' help with this process. Immune system disorders occur when the immune system does not fight tumours or harmful substances as it should. The immune response may be overactive or underactive.

REMEDY TO BOOST IMMUNITY

❖ Have tsp of honey with a pinch of turmeric and 5 mint leaves every morning. Do this all year round and it will really strengthen your immune system.

Iron Deficiency

Iron is essential to the body as it helps the entire body get oxygen and it is used to make haemoglobin. Anaemia, also known as iron deficiency, occurs when the body doesn't have sufficient iron. If your body doesn't have iron, it will make smaller and lesser red blood cells (RBCs). Then your body has less haemoglobin, and you cannot get enough oxygen.

What are the common causes of anaemia?

The most frequent cause of anaemia is a deficiency of iron, which is caused by low iron levels in the body. This occurs because you:

- ❖ suffer from dysmennorhoea
- ❖ are not getting enough iron in food; which can happen in people who need a lot of iron, such as small children, teens, and pregnant women;
- ❖ have internal bleeding, which may be caused by problems such as ulcers, haemorrhoids, or cancer. This bleeding can also happen with regular aspirin use. (Bleeding inside the body is the most common cause of iron deficiency anaemia in men and in women after menopause); and
- ❖ have a problem in iron absorption in your body, which is because of autoimmune disorders of the small intestine or a partial removal of the stomach or intestine.

You may not notice the symptoms of anaemia because it develops slowly and the symptoms may be mild. In fact, you may not notice them until your anaemia gets worse. As anaemia gets worse, you may:

- ❖ feel weak and tire out more easily
- ❖ feel dizzy
- ❖ be cranky
- ❖ have headaches
- ❖ look very pale
- ❖ feel short of breath
- ❖ have trouble concentrating

Foods and remedies to boost iron in the diet

Some foods have the ability to increase iron levels. If followed with regularity, the iron levels in your body will go up. Some of these foods are:

❖ Iron-rich foods include red meat, green leafy vegetables, cereals, eggs, seeds, dried fruit (especially apricots and dates), lentils, beans, and other pulses.

❖ Iron is better absorbed if you have some Vitamin C at the same time.

❖ Onions and garlic also help in iron absorption.

Note: Tea, coffee, and cola prevent iron absorption.

REMEDIES TO INCREASE IRON ABSORPTION
IN THE BODY

❖ Make a mix of onion seeds, black sesame, white sesame, cinnamon powder, dried mango powder, dried thyme, dried fenugreek leaves, and cumin seeds (equal proportions). Have 1 tsp of this mix after each meal to enhance iron absorption.

❖ Infuse a lemon in 2 litres of water and drink this through the day to enhance the absorption of iron.

Here are recipes of two delicious juices which help in the prevention of anaemia.

POPEYE'S BOOSTER

Ingredients

1 beet
10 spinach leaves
10 fenugreek seeds, soaked overnight
1 apple
A pinch of paprika
Honey to taste

Preparation

❖ Blend all the ingredients together.
❖ Drink immediately!

IRON MAN'S SECRET

Ingredients

20 black grapes
2 tomatoes
2 carrots
1 radish
2 celery stalks
Juice of 1 lime

Preparation

❖ Combine all the ingredients together.
❖ Drink fresh.

CALCIUM DEFICIENCY

Calcium is essential for us. Insufficient calcium intake can deplete calcium in the bones, thin and weaken bones and also lead to osteoporosis.

Hypocalcemia is a low level of calcium in the blood. It can occur from taking medications such as diuretics; it can also occur after certain medical treatments like thyroid and parathyroid surgery, etc.

An insufficient amount of calcium in your diet will generally not cause hypocalcemia. This is due to the fact that normal amounts of calcium in the blood are so significant to many fundamental body functions of the nerves, muscles, brain, and heart, that your body will draw calcium from the bones as needed to regulate normal blood calcium levels. This ensures that essential bodily processes are continued. Nonetheless, constant dietary calcium deficiency eventually leads to thinning of the bones and osteoporosis as the calcium reserves of the bones are not replaced by the body in time.

There are generally no symptoms of dietary calcium deficiency until bone thinning occurs and fractures develop in weakened bones. Symptoms can be vague, take years to develop, and may not be noticeable until advanced osteoporosis has developed. Symptoms can include:

❖ back or neck pain, which can be severe because of spinal bone fractures;
❖ bone pain;
❖ fracture that occurs with little or no trauma;
❖ loss of height; and

❖ stooped posture due to kyphosis (abnormal curving of the spine and humpback)

Symptoms of hypocalcemia, or low levels of calcium in the blood, are generally different from symptoms of dietary calcium deficiency. Some people may have no symptoms of hypocalcemia, while others may experience the following symptoms:

❖ muscle cramps
❖ numbness
❖ paresthesia (burning or prickling sensations)
❖ bleeding under the skin forming tiny red dots
❖ poor appetite
❖ purpura (large bruised areas)
❖ serious symptoms that might indicate a life-threatening condition

Calcium deficiency may occur with symptoms that might indicate a serious or life-threatening condition that should be immediately evaluated in an emergency setting. Seek immediate medical care if you have any of these life-threatening symptoms:

❖ change in level of consciousness or alertness, such as passing out (fainting) or unresponsiveness;
❖ chest pain, tightness, pressure, or heart palpitations;
❖ rapid, irregular or weak pulse;
❖ respiratory or breathing problems, such as shortness of breath, difficulty breathing, laboured breathing, wheezing, not breathing, or choking;

- seizure;
- tetany (muscle contractions, which can be sudden and painful); and
- unusual or profound weakness.

What are the causes of dietary calcium deficiency?

An important thing is that dietary calcium deficiency is due to the failure to ingest required amounts of calcium in the diet over a long period of time. Deficiencies of Vitamin D, phosphorous, and magnesium also cause calcium deficiency as they promote the absorption and use of calcium. Milk is a good sources of Vitamin D, phosphorous, and magnesium. When exposed to sunlight, your skin will produce Vitamin D.

What causes hypocalcemia?

Hypocalcemia can develop due to a variety of causes including:
- certain cancers, including breast and prostate cancer
- certain surgical procedures, such as the removal of the stomach
- hypoparathyroidism (low levels of parathyroid hormone, which regulates and maintains calcium and phosphorus levels)
- kidney failure
- medications and medical treatments, such as diuretics and chemotherapy

- pancreatitis (inflammation of the pancreas)
- sepsis (blood infection)
- Vitamin D, magnesium, or phosphate deficiency

Foods that increase calcium absorption

Like with iron deficiency, calcium deficiency is also manageable with a change in diet and by incorporating the following goods:
- Dairy foods like milk, cheese, and yoghurt are the richest sources.
- Green vegetables, soya and fish also contain calcium.
- Eat Vitamin C rich foods which help in calcium absorption.
- Zinc—found in chicken, mushrooms, pears, pineapples, cherries, dried figs, and dates—encourages acid production, which is necessary for calcium absorption.

REMEDIES FOR CALCIUM DEFICIENCY

- Make a mix of methi seeds, sesame seeds, flax seeds, caraway seeds, onion seeds, cumin seeds, and poppy seeds. Have 1 tsp of this at bedtime with 100 ml milk.

- Infuse 1 tbsp of fennel in 2 litres of water and drink through the day.

DEPRESSION

It is very easy to term a bad mood as 'depression'. You should
hope it isn't though. Medically, clinical depression is defined
as the mood disorder in which emotions of frustration,
sadness, anger and loss interrupt the daily life for weeks
or more.

Not surprisingly, the exact cause of depression is unknown.
Some researchers assume that it is due to chemical changes in
the brain, which occur because of a genetic problem or stressful
life events. Often, it's a combination of both. Some forms of
depression are hereditary. But depression can also occur if
you have no family history of the illness. Anyone can develop
depression, even kids.

The following may play a role in depression:
- ❖ alcohol or drug abuse
- ❖ certain medical conditions, including underactive thyroid,
  cancer, or long-term pain
- ❖ certain medications such as steroids
- ❖ sleeping problems
- ❖ stressful life events, such as:
  - • breaking up with a boyfriend or girlfriend
  - • failing in class
  - • financial stress
  - • death or illness of someone close to you
  - • divorce
  - • childhood abuse or neglect
  - • job loss
  - • social isolation (common in the elderly).

Depression can change or distort the way you see yourself, your life, and those around you. People who have depression usually see everything with a more negative attitude. They cannot imagine that any problem or situation can be solved in a positive way.

What are the symptoms of depression?

❖ feelings of sadness or unhappiness;
❖ irritability or frustration, even over small matters;
❖ lack of interest in normal activities;
❖ lack of libido;
❖ insomnia or excessive sleeping;
❖ appetite changes: depression causes both increased food cravings and loss of appetite in different people;
❖ indecisiveness and decreased concentration;
❖ fatigue—even small tasks may seem to require a lot of effort;
❖ feelings of worthlessness or guilt;
❖ trouble remembering things;
❖ crying spells for no apparent reason; and
❖ unexplained physical problems, such as back pain or headaches.

Depression symptoms affect people differently. For some, they are so severe that it's obvious that something is wrong. On the other hand, some people may just feel sad without knowing why.

Food that combat depression

There are some foods and eating habits which help combat depression. The following tips can be extremely helpful:

❖ The brain chemical, serotonin, enhances mood and the amino acid tryptophan helps boost serotonin levels. Tryptophan-rich foods include bread, bananas, dates, potatoes, and cauliflower.

❖ Higher serotonin levels help to lift your mood. Vitamin B6 found in meat, offal, chicken, wholegrain cereals, pulses, vegetables, nuts, and seeds is also needed for serotonin production.

❖ Eat a ripened banana every morning.

❖ Avoid alcohol and caffeine.

REMEDIES FOR DEPRESSION

❖ Make a mix of 2 tsp poppy seeds, 1 tsp star anise powder, ½ tsp crushed mace, 2 tsp flax meal and 1 tsp sesame seeds and have 1 tsp of this twice a day.

❖ Drink a minimum of 1 litre of water with ½ tsp elaichi powder and two star anise everyday between 11 am and 5 pm.

❖ Have a cup of chamomile tea and 2 walnuts, 1 tsp melon or pumpkin seeds every evening.

❖ Eat 1 tsp chironji (cuddapah nuts) at bedtime.

MENOPAUSE

Menopause is the most dreaded period of a woman's life. During menopause, a woman's ovaries stop producing eggs and they produce less oestrogen and progesterone. Changes in these hormones cause menopause symptoms. Periods occur less often and eventually stop. Sometimes this happens suddenly. But most of the time, periods gradually stop over time. Menopause is complete when you have not had a period for one year.

What are the common symptoms of menopause?

Symptoms vary from woman to woman. They may last five or more years. Some women may have worse symptoms than others. Common symptoms of menopause include:

❖ menstrual periods that occur less often and eventually stop
❖ heart pounding or racing
❖ hot flashes, usually worst during the first one or two years
❖ night sweats
❖ skin flushing
❖ sleeping problems (insomnia)

Other symptoms of menopause may include:

❖ forgetfulness (in some women)
❖ headaches
❖ decreased interest in sex, possibly decreased response to sexual stimulation
❖ irritability, depression, and anxiety
❖ excessive need to urinate
❖ vaginal dryness and painful sexual intercourse

133

❖ vaginal infections
❖ joint aches and pains

When menopause happens before the age of 40, it is considered early. Early menopause is due to some specific medical treatments and can also happen on its own.

Foods that help during menopause

There are foods and dietary tips which help in reliving the symptoms of menopause. Some of them are as follows:
❖ Eat oestrogen foods like soya beans, tofu, seaweed, and flaxseed for the phyto-oestrogens they contain.
❖ Fruits like plums, apples, bananas, cherries, papaya, and pomegranates.
❖ Vegetables like beetroot and broccoli.
❖ Ensure a good calcium intake.
❖ The essential fatty acids Omega 3 and Omega 6 help to protect against heart disease, keep the skin supple, and the joints mobile. Eat oily fish, nuts, and seeds.

REMEDIES TO EASE OUT MENOPAUSE

❖ Make a mix of flax meal, curry leaf powder, bay leaves, pepper powder, sesame seeds, cumin seeds, cloves, turmeric powder and cumin. Have 2 tsp of this after lunch and dinner.

❖ Infuse 3 roasted bay leaves in 1 litre of water and drink this through the day

MEMORY LOSS

Almost all of us tend to forget things. However, sometimes it takes extreme forms like dementia and Alzheimer's. It can be caused by many factors.

What are the common causes of memory loss?

❖ **Medications**: A number of prescription and over-the-counter medications can interfere with or cause loss of memory. Antidepressants, antihistamines, anti-anxiety medications, muscle relaxants, tranquilizers, sleeping pills, and pain medications given after surgery can cause it.

❖ **Alcohol, tobacco, or drug use**: Excessive alcohol use has long been recognized as a cause of memory loss.

❖ **Smoking**: This habit harms the memory by reducing the amount of oxygen that gets to the brain. Illicit drugs can change chemicals in the brain, which can make it hard to recall memories.

❖ **Sleep deprivation**: Both quantity and quality of sleep are important to memory. Not getting adequate sleep leads to extreme fatigue and interferes with the ability to comprehend and remember information.

❖ **Nutritional deficiency**: Proper nutrition is essential for brain function. Vitamins B1 and B12 deficiencies can affect memory.

❖ **Head injury**: If there occurs a severe head injury, it can cause long term and short term memory loss.

❖ **Stroke**: A stroke can cause short term memory loss.

- ❖ **Dementia**: Dementia is the name for progressive loss of memory and other aspects of thinking that are severe enough to interfere with the ability to function in daily activities.
- ❖ **Other causes**: Other possible causes of memory loss include an underactive or overactive thyroid gland and infections such as HIV, tuberculosis, and syphilis that affects the brain.

Foods that combat memory loss

To combat memory loss, you need to especially work on your nutrition and the food. Some things to be remembered are:

- ❖ Eat foods rich in antioxidants like grapes, cherries, and berries.
- ❖ Eat Vitamin E-rich foods like apples, broccoli, eggs, nuts, and seeds.
- ❖ Eat foods rich in B complex like liver, yeast, and wholegrain; and
- ❖ Avoid Aspartame.

REMEDIES FOR MEMORY LOSS

- ❖ Have 1 tbsp of honey with 5 strands of saffron and 1 walnut daily.

- ❖ Make a mix of 2 tsp flax meal, ¼ tsp turmeric powder, 10 strands of saffron, 1 tsp poppy seeds, 2 tsp fennel, ½ tsp dried basil, 2 tsp cumin, ¼ tsp cinnamon, and 2 tsp dried coriander. Eat 1 tsp of this after breakfast.

❖ Have 5 almonds and 1 walnut with 1 tsp honey and a pinch of rosemary.

❖ Eat 2 dried figs and 2 peppercorns with a drop of cow's ghee at bedtime.

❖ Brew 1 tsp black cumin seeds and 1 tsp dried sage in 200 ml water and drink this every morning.

7

Stomach Issues

WHAT IS THE BIGGEST DETERRENT IN EATING EVERYTHING YOU love? Yes, you guessed it right. Stomach issues. Be it diarrhoea, constipation, acidity, or indigestion, the first thing it affects is what we eat. Khichdi is definitely not your favourite meal—believe me it isn't mine either.

The worst thing that can happen to the stomach is IBS, which happened to a client of mine. IBS is a mixture of acidity, indigestion, constipation, and diarrhoea. Yep, every stomach's nightmare.

Thirsty-five-year old Sheena was diagnosed with IBS when she was 31, just after the birth of her son. She had gone through a very stressful gestation period and initially thought that her symptoms were because of that. It was only when her weight dropped to 37 kg that she got worried and visited her doctor.

When Sheena first met me she had lost another 2 kg and was weighing a miserly 35 kg with a BMI of 16.2. She was not able to function properly and had lost her zest for life. She was scared each time she ate a meal and would spend the next couple of hours agonizing over whether it would cause her abdominal cramps, or flatulence, or diarrhoea, or constipation. One of her friends suggested that she meet me. I asked her to put down her dietary recall and was amazed to find that she had eliminated most foods from her diet and was subsisting only on soft cooked rice and doodhi sabji. She complained that her weight loss and stomach issues were stressing her so much that she would not sleep at night. Her little baby was being looked after by maids and a nanny, and this distressed her even more.

The first thing I had to do was to increase Sheena's confidence and encourage her to gradually start incorporating more foods in her diet. This was easier said than done. Over the years Sheena had suffered so much abdominal distress that she was not inclined to upset the balance by eating any other foods. I explained to her that if she carried on like this it would be detrimental to her health and suggested that we would take baby steps toward ensuring good health. To instill confidence in her, I told her that she could reach out to me any time of the day or night via phone calls, messages, emails, and BBM!

The mix I gave her included dried mint, dried thyme, ajwain, dried tulsi, white sesame, jeera, saffron, and khus khus. I asked her to take just 1 tsp of this powder immediately after her meals. Initially, she was very apprehensive and would call four to five times a day. This process continued for a month. When we met again she had gained a kilo but was still afraid that she would get pain or gas if she ate more food. I explained that if she was not relaxed at meal times, she would definitely not be able to digest her food well, and this could happen to even those without IBS. There were times I had to be stern with her and then there were times I had to handle her with kid gloves. Slowly she started eating a wider variety of foods but she still avoided gluten-rich foods. She also started taking 2 tsp of the mix after meals. Her weight increased by another 2.3 kg after two months. Her happiest moment came four months later when she ate a regular thali and digested it well!

Now all of us don't want to be like Sheena. So here's what you can do. Read on and keep the remedy handy to use whenever needed. All of it is right here, at your service!

DIARRHOEA

Diarrhoea is generally when bowel movements (stool) are loose and watery. It is usually not serious. Many people will inevitably suffer from diarrhoea once or twice each year. It typically lasts two to three days and can be treated with over-the-counter medicines. Some people have diarrhoea often as part of IBS or other chronic diseases of the large intestine.

What are the symptoms of diarrhoea?

Symptoms of diarrhoea can be broken down into uncomplicated (or non-serious) diarrhoea and complicated diarrhoea. Complicated diarrhoea may be a sign of a more serious illness.

Symptoms of uncomplicated diarrhoea include:

❖ abdominal bloating or cramps
❖ thin or loose stool
❖ watery stool
❖ urgency to have a bowel movement
❖ nausea and vomiting

In addition to the symptoms described above, the symptoms of complicated diarrhoea include:

❖ blood, mucous, or undigested food in the stool
❖ weight loss
❖ fever

What causes diarrhoea?

Diarrhoea happens when what you eat and drink is expelled from your body much too quickly or in too large amounts. In normal conditions, the liquids from the food you ingest in absorbed by the colon leaving a semi solid stool, but if the liquids aren't absorbed by the colon, the result is a watery bowel movement.

A number of diseases and conditions can cause diarrhoea. Common causes of diarrhoea include:

❖ **Viruses**: Viruses that can cause diarrhoea include the Norwalk virus and the cytomegalo virus. Acute childhood diarrhoea is often caused by rotavirus. Viral hepatitis is another common cause of diarrhoea.
❖ **Bacteria and parasites**: that are present in contaminated food or water can transmit bacteria and parasites to your

body. Diarrhoea caused by bacteria and parasites can be common when travelling.

❖ **Medications**: Many medications can cause diarrhoea. The most common are antibiotics. Antibiotics destroy both good and bad bacteria, which can disturb the natural balance of bacteria in your intestines.

❖ **Lactose intolerance**: It is caused because the body stops making the required enzyme to digest lactose after childhood. Hence, people who are lactose intolerant have a difficulty in digestion and experience diarrhoea after consumption of dairy products. Lactose intolerance increases with age.

❖ **Fructose**: Fructose, a sugar found naturally in fruits and honey and added as a sweetener to some beverages, can cause diarrhoea in people who have trouble digesting it.

❖ **Artificial sweeteners**: Sorbitol and mannitol, artificial sweeteners found in chewing gum and other sugar-free products, can cause diarrhoea in some otherwise healthy people.

❖ **Surgery**: Some people may experience diarrhoea after undergoing abdominal surgery or gall bladder removal surgery.

❖ **Other digestive disorders**: Chronic diarrhoea has a number of other causes, such as Crohn's Disease, ulcerative colitis, celiac disease, microscopic colitis, and IBS.

REMEDY FOR PROPER BOWEL MOVEMENT

Ingredients

Powder ¼ tsp grated nutmeg
1 tsp jeera
1 tsp saunf
¼ tsp soonth

Preparation

❖ Make a paste with 2 tbsp of water and consume thrice a day. Now, this paste may make you feel sleepy, so ensure that you get adequate rest. Also drink plenty of water to rehydrate your system. Your diarrhoea will soon vanish.

CONSTIPATION

Constipation means different things to different people. For many people, it simply means infrequent bowel movement. For others, however, constipation means hard stool, difficulty passing stools, or a sense of incomplete emptying after a bowel movement.

Constipation usually is defined as fewer than three bowel movements per week. As there is no medical reason for a daily bowel movement, severe constipation is defined by less than one bowel movement in one week. There is no physical discomfort caused by an absence of bowel movement for two to three days; however people do experience mental discomfort.

It is important to distinguish acute constipation from chronic constipation. Acute constipation requires urgent assessment because a serious medical illness may be the underlying cause (for example, tumours of the colon). Constipation also requires an immediate assessment if it is accompanied by troubling symptoms such as rectal bleeding, abdominal pain and cramps, nausea and vomiting, and involuntary loss of weight.

What are the causes of constipation?

Causes of constipation can be very varied. Here are some of the most common ones:

* **Habit**: Bowel movements are under voluntary control. This means that the normal urge people feel when they need to have a bowel movement can be suppressed. Although occasionally it is appropriate to suppress an urge to defecate (for example, when a bathroom is not available!), doing this too frequently can lead to a disappearance of urges and result in constipation.
* **Diet**: Low fibre diets often lead to constipation as fibre is essential in maintaining a soft stool. Fruits, vegetables and whole grains are the best natural sources of fibre.
* **Hormonal disorders**: Hormones can affect bowel movements too. For example:

- too little thyroid hormone (hypothyroidism) and too much parathyroid hormone (by raising the calcium levels in the blood) can cause constipation;
- at the time of a woman's menstrual periods, oestrogen and progesterone levels are high and may cause constipation. However, this is rarely a prolonged problem; and
- high levels of oestrogen and progesterone during pregnancy can also cause constipation.

❖ **Diseases of the colon**: There are many diseases that can affect the function of the muscles and/or nerves of the colon. These include diabetes, scleroderma, intestinal pseudo-obstruction, Hirschsprung's disease, and Chagas disease. Cancer or narrowing of the colon that blocks the colon likewise can cause a decrease in the flow of stool.

❖ **Pelvic floor dysfunction**: Pelvic floor dysfunction refers to a condition in which the muscles of the lower pelvis that surround the rectum (the pelvic floor muscles) do not work normally. These muscles are critical for bowel movement.

What are the symptoms of constipation?

Not having a bowel movement every day doesn't necessarily mean you're constipated. You probably have constipation, however, if you've had at least two of the following signs and symptoms for at least three of the past six months:

❖ bowel movement less than three times a week
❖ experience hard stools
❖ strain excessively during bowel movement

❖ experience a sense of rectal blockage
❖ need to use manual manoeuvres for bowel movement, such as using a finger or manipulation of your lower abdomen

How can constipation be prevented and treated?

There are several things you can do to prevent constipation. Some of them are:

❖ Eat a well balanced, fibre-rich diet. Good sources of fibre are fruits, vegetables, legumes, and wholegrain bread and cereal (especially bran). Fibre and water help the colon pass stool.
❖ Drink 1½ to 2 litres of water and other fluids. Liquids that contain caffeine, such as coffee and soft drinks, have a dehydrating effect. Some people may need to avoid milk, as dairy products may be constipating for them.
❖ Exercise regularly.

REMEDIES FOR CONSTIPATION

❖ Eat 2 dates or 2 figs at bedtime with a warm glass of water.

❖ Eat a mix of flaxseed powder and chia seeds post lunch and dinner to ease bowel movement.

❖ A mix of flax seeds, coriander seeds, and mint powder taken thrice a day will also help.

ACIDITY

Acidity is probably the most uncomfortable ailment to have. It gives you gas, chest pains, which make you unable to eat or sit properly. The stomach normally secretes acid that is essential in the digestive process. This acid helps in breaking down food during digestion. When there is excess production of acid by the gastric glands of the stomach, it results in the condition known as acidity. Acidity is responsible for symptoms like dyspepsia, heartburn, and the formation of ulcers (erosion of the lining of the stomach or intestines).

Acidity tends to have a much higher incidence in highly emotional and nervous individuals. Consumption of alcohol, extremely spicy foods, and non-vegetarian diets also increase the chances of getting acidity.

What are the causes of acidity?

The stomach, intestines, and digestive glands secrete hydrochloric acid and various enzymes, including pepsin, that break down and digest food. The stomach must also be protected from the same acid and enzymes, or it too can be attacked by the gastric juices. The acid may enter the lower part of the oesophagus due to some weakness in the normal sphincter mechanism that prevents such reflux. This causes heartburn.

Ulcers also occur as a result of over secretion of acid. This may happen when there is an imbalance between the digestive juices used by the stomach to break down food and the various factors that protect the lining of the stomach and duodenum (the part of the small intestine that adjoins the stomach).

What are the symptoms and signs of acidity?

Dyspepsia and heartburn are often the main symptoms of acidity. Heartburn is characterized by stabbing pain in the chest behind the sternum (breast bone). This occurs after meals and can be induced by excessive intra abdominal pressure like during weight lifting. Heartburn also occurs at night when you are lying down and is relieved immediately once you sit up. This pain is interlinked with the body posture. Ulcers are symptomized by either localized or diffused pain. Sometimes the pain reaches your back too.

The most frequent symptom is dyspepsia which can be described as a burning pain in the upper area of the abdomen. Very rarely, there is no pain but just a feeling of indigestion and nausea.

More commonly, acidity occurs when your diet is affected. So eating properly is imperative. Taking long gaps between meals or an erratic eating cycle causes acidity.

What is the treatment of acidity?

Once again, at the cost of repeating myself, diet is the most important cure for acidity. It is important to eat right, at the right time. Here are some tips on how to prevent and cure acidity:
❖ Drink plenty of water.

❖ Avoid long gaps between meals.
❖ Spicy and fried foods are a definite no.
❖ Also avoid certain foods that trigger reflux like raw sprouts, chillies, paprika, peppers, steak, and eggs.

REMEDY FOR ACIDITY

Have soaked black raisins, a glass of doodhi juice, and 10 soaked methi seeds every day.

INDIGESTION

Indigestion—also called dyspepsia or an upset stomach—is a general term that describes discomfort in your upper abdomen. Indigestion is not a disease, but rather a collection of symptoms you experience, including bloating, belching, and nausea. It is a term used to describe a feeling of fullness or discomfort during or after a meal. It can be accompanied by burning or pain in the upper stomach. Although indigestion is common, how you experience indigestion may differ from person to person.

What are the symptoms of indigestion?

❖ bloating (feeling full)
❖ belching and gas

❖ nausea and vomiting
❖ sour taste
❖ growling stomach
❖ burning in the stomach or upper abdomen
❖ abdominal pain

These symptoms may increase in times of stress.

People often have heartburn along with indigestion. But heartburn is caused by stomach acids rising into the oesophagus.

What are the causes and risks of indigestion?

Remember, people of all ages and of both sexes are affected by indigestion and it's extremely common. An individual's risk increases with excess alcohol consumption, use of drugs that may irritate the stomach (such as aspirin), other conditions where there is an abnormality in the digestive tract, such as an ulcer, and emotional problems such as anxiety or depression.

Indigestion has many causes, including:
❖ Diseases:
  • ulcers
  • gastroesophageal reflux disease (GERD)
  • stomach cancer (rare)
  • gastroparesis (a condition where the stomach doesn't empty properly; this often occurs in diabetics)
  • stomach infections
  • IBS
  • chronic pancreatitis
  • thyroid disease

❖ Lifestyle:
  • eating too much, eating too fast, eating high-fat foods, or eating during stressful situations
  • drinking too much alcohol
  • smoking
  • stress and fatigue

How can indigestion be prevented?

The best way to prevent indigestion is to avoid the foods and situations that seem to cause indigestion. Keeping a food diary is helpful in identifying foods that cause indigestion. Here are some other suggestions:

❖ Eat small meals so the stomach does not have to work as hard or as long.
❖ Eat slowly. Chew your food well.
❖ Avoid foods that contain high amounts of acids, such as citrus fruits and tomatoes.
❖ Reduce or avoid foods and beverages that contain caffeine.
❖ If stress is a trigger for your indigestion, re-evaluating your lifestyle may help to reduce stress.
❖ Smokers should consider quitting smoking, or at least not smoking right before or after eating, as smoking can irritate the stomach lining.
❖ Cut back on alcohol consumption.
❖ Avoid wearing tight-fitting garments because they tend to compress the stomach.
❖ Do not exercise with a full stomach. Rather, exercise before a meal or at least one hour after eating a meal.

❖ Do not lie down right after eating.
❖ Wait at least three hours after your last meal of the day before going to bed.

REMEDY FOR INDIGESTION

Make a mix of jeera, saunf, black salt, and tulsi and eat 1 tsp of this after each meal. Indigestion will vanish. Poof!

PILES

Piles are actually inflamed haemorrhoids. Haemorrhoids can be defined as masses of tissue in the anal canal, which are full of blood vessels, support tissue, muscle, and elastic fibres. Haemorrhoids as unpleasant inflammations, but we all have them. The problem occurs when these haemorrhoids become too big. Piles are the swollen haemorrhoids that are painful and cause problems. Piles can be of various sizes and may be internal (inside the anus) or external ones (outside the anus). The internal ones are much more common.

What are the symptoms of piles?

An individual with piles may experience the following symptoms:

❖ a hard lump may be felt around the anus. It consists of coagulated blood. This can be extremely painful;
❖ feeling that the bowels are still full after going to the toilet;
❖ bright red blood during a bowel movement;
❖ itchiness in the anus area;
❖ mucus discharge when emptying the bowels;
❖ pain while defecating;
❖ the anus area may be red and sore; and
❖ when passing a stool the person may strain excessively.

What are the causes?

Piles is caused because the blood vessels around the anus and in the rectum will stretch under pressure and may swell or bulge. Inflamed veins (haemorrhoids) can develop when pressure increases in the lower rectum. This may be due to:
❖ anal intercourse
❖ chronic constipation
❖ chronic diarrhoea
❖ lifting heavy weights regularly
❖ being overweight
❖ pregnancy
❖ sitting on the toilet for too long
❖ straining when passing a stool

Food that can ease piles

Diet can be a very effective way of curbing the risk of piles and reducing the frequency of their occurrence. The following tips can be kept in mind:

❖ Eat fibre-rich foods like fresh fruits (bananas, papaya, chickoos, and berries) and vegetables (drumsticks, leafy vegetables, gourds), chickpeas, beans, oats, and muesli.

❖ Drink a minimum of 2.5 litres of water daily to keep your bowel contents bulky.

REMEDIES FOR PILES

❖ Make a mix of flax meal, fennel, dried coriander powder, cumin powder, and white sesame seeds. Eat 2 tsp of this after lunch and dinner.

❖ Add 1 tbsp of sabjia takmakia seeds or basil seeds generally used in faloodas to a litre of water. It will provide the pectin needed to keep the bowel movement soft.

❖ Chew on 1 tbsp of flaxseed at night.

❖ You can split a cup of warm cow's milk with the juice of 1 lime. Add 1 tsp fennel powder to this coagulate (chenna) and ingest on an empty stomach every morning. Do this daily for one week, then repeat whenever needed.

❖ Onion juice with radish juice and honey also helps cure bleeding piles. Consume this every night for a week or until the bleeding stops.

8

Skin and Hair Issues

HOW OFTEN WE LOOK AT THE MODELS AND ACTRESSES ON television or in ads and feel envious about their flawless skin and beautiful hair? We all secretly want that. I often find myself touching my hair or feeling my skin in response to those ads. Some of it is make-up, sure, but the rest of it is good skin care. Now by skin care I don't mean the products these women advertise. I mean good diet and quick home remedies. Yes. You'll be amazed to find how religiously people follow such things, and well, the results are there for us all to see.

So, here you go. Surprise yourselves and discover how much good you yourself can do for you!

DRY SKIN

The cause of dry skin is less oil production by the sebaceous glands of the skin. Dry skin can be a temporary problem, like something that you get in the cold weather, or it may be a lifelong issue.

If you have dry skin, you're likely to experience one or more of the following:

* a feeling of skin tightness, especially after showering, bathing, or swimming
* skin that appears dehydrated
* skin that feels and looks rough rather than smooth
* itching
* flaking
* fine lines or cracks
* redness

Some reasons for dry skin are environmental factors like dry climate, sun exposure, and pollution, and these you can't change. But, of course, make-up, harsh soaps, and improper nutrition are the factors you can work on. Did you know deficiencies of Vitamins A, C, and E can also cause dry skin?

What are the potential causes of dry skin?

* **The weather**: In general, your skin is driest in winter, when temperatures and humidity levels plummet. Winter conditions also tend to make many existing skin conditions worse. But the reverse may be true if you live in arid regions, where temperatures soar, but humidity levels remain low.
* **Appliances**: Air conditioning, wood burning stoves, space

heaters and fireplaces dry the skin because they reduce humidity.

❖ **Long baths**: If you are one of those people who takes a long, hot bath you will have dry skin. Frequent showering and swimming breaks down the lipid barriers of your skin.

❖ **Deodarants, antibacterial soaps, etc.**: and other soaps and detergents take away lipids and water from your skin. Harsh shampoos dry out your scalp too.

❖ **Exposure to the sun**: Sun exposure dries up your skin. However, damage from UV rays penetrates more than just the top layer of skin. The maximum damage is done deep inside the dermis, where the elastic fibres and collagen break down at a much quicker pace, resulting in deep wrinkles and loose, sagging skin. This sun damaged skin gives the appearance of dry skin.

Food that helps combat dry skin

A healthy and nutritious diet proves helpful in treating every ailment, including dry skin. A good dry skin preventative diet should include three main categories:

❖ **Water-based**: Choose water-based fruits and vegetables for added hydration. This includes items such as cantaloupe, grapes, oranges, celery, cucumbers, tomatoes, green peepers, and onions.

❖ **Vitamin-packed**: Choose foods high in Vitamins A, B, and C and in natural antioxidants for skin renewal and repair. These foods include selections such as apricots, strawberries, carrots, blueberries, orange and yellow vegetables like squash and carrots, leafy green vegetables like spinach, and raw milk products or plain yoghurt.

❖ **Sulphur-containing**: Choose foods that are high in sulphur content to promote skin rejuvenation. Eggs, garlic, and asparagus are great choices for this category.

REMEDIES FOR DRY SKIN

Sometimes, even after taking all the preventative measures, you can't prevent dry skin. For such cases, there are several natural home remedies that can come to your rescue. Here are a few of them that can easily be incorporated into your daily routine.

❖ Apply a pack of whole milk mixed with 1 tsp of almond paste, and wash after 15 to 20 minutes with cold water.

❖ Apply mashed avocado mixed with a few drops of fresh lime juice and olive oil on the skin and wash after 15 to 20 minutes.

❖ Apply mashed banana with 1 tsp of honey on the face, keep for 15 minutes, and rinse off with cold water for an instant glow.

❖ Massage the skin with a combination of rose oil and almond oil every night before going to bed. Your skin will stay very soft and supple.

❖ Apply aloe vera gel on skin to nourish and hydrate it.

❖ Regularly use a pack made from 1 egg yolk, 1 tsp oatmeal, and 1 tbsp rose water to prevent wrinkles.

❖ Use a mask made from tomato and papaya paste. Leave it on for 20 minutes, and rinse off with cold water.

❖ Ensure that you drink sufficient water to hydrate the skin.

Use these remedies regularly and eat healthy, and dry skin will be a long-forgotten problem!

OILY SKIN

Oily skin. Our personal demon. No, it doesn't give our skin a glow; it makes it shiny, thick, and dull coloured. Very often oily skin has open pores and pimples and other embarrassing forms of acne. This type of skin is also prone to blackheads. The reason for the oiliness is that the oil generating sebaceous glands are overactive and produce a lot more oil than needed. The oil oozes out and gives the skin a greasy shine. The pores are enlarged and the skin has a coarse look. And hence, we all hate it.

Causes of oily skin

❖ heredity
❖ diet

- ❖ hormone levels
- ❖ pregnancy
- ❖ birth control pills
- ❖ cosmetics
- ❖ humidity and hot weather

Because of the hormonal shifts of adolescence, oily skin is common in teenagers, but it can occur at any age, as many of us will attest. In general, skin tends to become drier with age. The flow of sebum or oil increases during adolescence and starts decreasing with age. During pregnancy and menopause, hormonal imbalances can also upset the oil balance and increase the activity of sebaceous glands, which results in oily skin. However, oily skin is advantageous as it doesn't age as fast as other skin types.

Food that combat oily skin

The correct diet is an essential part of treating any disease, and any issue with our body. The same goes for oily skin. You can treat your oily skin with the right foods and of course some homemade packs and scrubs. But the following is essential.

- ❖ A diet rich in proteins but restricted in sugar, fluids, and salt.
- ❖ Eat plenty of leafy green vegetables and fresh fruits.
- ❖ Even a slight deficiency in Vitamin B2 can cause oily skin. Nutritional yeast, wheatgerm, and organ meats provide both Vitamins B5 and B2. Other good sources of Vitamin

B2 are wholegrains, beans, and nuts. Buckwheat, black beans, and whole rice are excellent to supply the body with iron and rejuvenate pale skin.

❖ Drink plenty of quality water to keep the skin hydrated and flush out toxins.

❖ Reduce the amount of fat in your diet. Avoid pork and fried and highly seasoned foods. consume no animal fats, or heat-processed vegetable oils.

REMEDIES FOR OILY SKIN

❖ Make a pack of 2 tbsp rice flour, 1 tbsp besan, 1 tsp lemon rind, 2 tsp lemon juice, and 2 tsp rose water. Apply on gently on your face. Leave for 2 minutes and then rinse off with cold water.

❖ To reduce blackheads: use a scrub made of 2 tbsp oatmeal, ¼ tsp haldi powder, and 2 tbsp lemon juice. Use this to cleanse you face.

❖ Use equal parts of honey and rose water to soothe the skin if it is oily. Just apply and leave on for an hour, rinse with water, and then dab cotton wool dipped in milk all over the face. Keep on for 10 minutes and then rinse off with cold water. You can rub an ice cube all over your face after this for even better results

ACNE

Acne is not dangerous, but can leave skin scars—and emotional scars. All of us have, at one point of time, had for those ugly red pimples, and not quite known how to handle it. Curing acne is important not just for your skin, but for yourself too. And the first step of curing is knowing what exactly is acne.

Pimples have the tendency to appear on the face, back, chest, shoulders and neck in humans. In layman's language, when skin cells, sebum and hair clump together into a plug that gets infected by bacteria it becomes a swelling. A pimple develops when this plug breaks.

There are various types of pimples:

❖ **Whiteheads** are those which are miniscule and remain under the skin

❖ **Blackheads** are clearly visible, black bumps which appear on the skin. Since a blackhead is not caused by dirt, scrubbing your face rigorously when you see a blackhead won't help.

❖ **Papules** are usually pink small bumps which are visible on the surface of the skin.

❖ **Pustules** are clearly visible on the surface of the skin. They are red at their base and have pus at the top.

❖ **Nobules** are clearly visible on the surface of the skin. They are large, solid pimples, painful, and embedded deep in the skin.

❖ **Cysts** are clearly visible on the surface of the skin. They are painful, and are filled with pus. Cysts can easily cause scars.

Measures to control acne

Looking after your skin if you have acne (or are prone to acne) includes the following measures:

* ❖ Do not wash your face more than twice a day, and that too only with a mild soap especially made for people with acne. Use warm water and try not to scrub the skin.
* ❖ Don't try to burst the pimples. This in fact pushes the infection further down causing heightened blocking, even worse swelling and redness. It is also increases scarring.
* ❖ Avoid touching your face with your hands. Ensure that the receiver of the phone doesn't touch your face when you are talking, as it may have sebum and skin residue on it.
* ❖ Keep your hands clean, wash them regularly.
* ❖ Glasses should be cleaned regularly. They will collect sebum (skin oil) and skin residue.
* ❖ Your skin needs air, and hence if you have acne on your back, shoulders, and chest you should wear loose fitting clothing. Definitely avoid wearing tight garments.
* ❖ Don't go to sleep with make-up on.
* ❖ Hair collects sebum and skin residue. Keep your hair clean and away from your face.
* ❖ Too much sun can cause your skin to produce more sebum. Several acne medications make it more likely that you will be sunburned.
* ❖ If you shave your face, do it carefully. Use either an electric shaver or safety razors. If you use a safety razor, make sure the blade is sharp. Soften your skin/beard with warm soapy water before applying the shaving cream.

What can make acne worse?

I know you're thinking that it's already bad, and what do you mean by making it worse, but well there are certain things that do actually make acne worse. There are certain things we can do nothing about, but there are some which we can change, like lifestyle. So remember these:

❖ **Menstrual cycle:** Girls and women with acne tend to get it worse one or two weeks before their menstrual period arrives. This is probably due to hormonal changes that take place. Some people say they eat more chocolate during this time and wonder whether there may be a connection. However, experts believe the worsening acne is not due to chocolate, but rather to hormonal changes.

❖ **Anxiety and stress:** When you are stressed out, the levels of cortisol and adrenaline rise, making the acne worse.

❖ **Hot and humid climate:** When it is hot and humid we sweat more. This can make the acne worse.

❖ **Oil-based cosmetics:** Moisturizing creams, lubricating lotions, and all make-up that contain oil can speed up the blocking of your pores.

❖ **Greasy hair:** Some hair products are very greasy and might have the same effect as oil-based make-up. Hair products with cocoa butter or coconut butter are some examples.

REMEDIES FOR ACNE

Don't lose hope as yet. Pimples are horrible and scarring and they are known as *Acne vulgaris* for a reason. But here are two solid remedies that will make them go away, and fast!

❖ Make a face pack using 2 tsp dried orange peel, 10 mint leaves, the juice of 1 lemon, and 2 tbsp grated cucumber. Leave on the face for an hour. Then wash with cold water.

❖ To prevent pimples from leaving scars, peel a clove of garlic, squash it, and rub the clove of garlic on the pimple. Allow the juice to act for 10 minutes and then rinse with cold water.

HAIR

Beautiful hair has always been an asset to us Indians, hasn't it? Very often we take it for granted. Hair is made of a protein called keratin. All that protein-rich food is necessary for proper growth of our hair. It goes through so many problems: hair loss, dandruff, oily hair, frizzy hair, and what not. We are so caught up in our lives that we don't spare the time to treat our hair with the care it deserves. The constant use of chemicals, and the dust...our hair cries and we never hear it! We'll take a look at some of those many problems in this part.

Hair Loss

Hair loss is a common problem faced by millions of people all over the world. Many of us are worried when our hair begins thinning, lessening, or disappearing, as it affects our appearance. There can be several causes or reasons for hair loss.

What are the signs and symptoms of hair loss?

* **Gradual thinning on top of head**: This is the most common type of hair loss, affecting both men and women. In men, hair often begins to recede from the forehead in a line that resembles the letter M. Women typically retain a line of hair at the forehead but experience a broadening of the parting in their hair, especially if it's a centre parting.
* **Circular or patchy bald spots**: Some people experience smooth bald spots, often about an inch across. This type of hair loss usually affects just the scalp, but it sometimes also occurs in beards or eyebrows. In some cases, your skin may become itchy or painful before the hair falls out.
* **Sudden loosening of hair**: A physical or emotional shock can cause hair loss. Handfuls of hair may come out when combing or washing your hair or even after gentle tugging. This type of hair loss usually causes overall hair thinning and not bald patches.
* **Full-body hair loss**: Some conditions and medical treatments, such as chemotherapy for cancer, can result in the loss of hair all over your body. The hair usually grows back after treatment ends.

Most people normally shed fifty to hundred strands of hair a day. But with about 100,000 hairs in the scalp, this amount of hair loss shouldn't cause noticeable thinning of the scalp hair. As people age, hair tends to gradually thin. Other causes of hair loss include hormonal factors, medical conditions, and medications.

Hormonal factors

The most common cause of hair loss is a hereditary condition called male-pattern baldness or female-pattern baldness. In genetically susceptible people, certain sex hormones trigger a particular pattern of permanent hair loss. Most common in men, this type of hair thinning can begin as early as puberty. Hormonal changes and imbalances can also cause temporary hair loss. This could be due to pregnancy, childbirth, discontinuation of birth control pills, or the onset of menopause.

Medical conditions

A variety of medical conditions can cause hair loss, including:
* **Thyroid problems:** The thyroid gland helps regulate hormone levels in your body. If the gland isn't working properly, hair loss may result;
* **Alopecia areata:** This disease occurs when the body's immune system attacks hair follicles, causing smooth, roundish patches of hair loss;
* **Scalp infections:** Infections such as ringworm can invade

the hair and skin of your scalp, leading to hair loss. Once infections are treated, hair generally grows back.

* **Other skin disorders**: Diseases that can cause scarring, such as lichen planus and some types of lupus, can result in permanent hair loss where the scars occur.

Medications

Hair loss can be caused by drugs used to treat:
* cancer
* arthritis
* depression
* heart problems
* high blood pressure

Other causes of hair loss

Hair loss can also result from:
* **Hair-pulling disorder**: This mental illness causes people to have an irresistible urge to pull out their hair, whether it's from the scalp, their eyebrows, or other areas of the body. Hair pulling from the scalp often leaves patchy bald spots on the head;
* **Certain hairstyles**: Traction hair loss can occur if the hair is pulled too tightly into hairstyles such as pigtails or cornrows.

Foods that combat hair loss

A balanced diet with proper amounts of seeds, nuts, fruits, vegetables, and grains is very important for healthy hair growth.

Consuming more proteins by way of milk, buttermilk, soybean, wheatgerm, etc. are very good for hair health. The following are a few important essentials in terms of diet while keeping in mind hair loss:

- ❖ **Omega-3 Fatty Acids:** Foods packed with Omega-3 fatty acids promote scalp health and prevent your hair from appearing dull and lifeless. Salmon, in particular, is loaded with Omega-3s and also supplies you with Vitamin B-12 and iron. One tablespoon or two of ground flaxseed added to your diet will also ensure you are taking in these essential fatty acids. Blend ground flax seed into your morning milkshake for a quick boost.

- ❖ **Vitamins E, A, C, D, and K**: Extra virgin olive oil contains Vitamins E, A, D, and K, all of which aid hair growth. It can easily be drizzled over any meal or snack. Known for its conditioning and antioxidant properties, extra virgin olive oil can function as a topical agent; you can apply it directly to your hair. Dark green vegetables such as spinach and broccoli are rich in Vitamins A and C, which help your body produce the sebum that is secreted by hair follicles and naturally conditions your locks. Carrots deliver the Vitamin A that your hair needs.

- ❖ **Silica**: Although silica is found in the skins of potatoes and cucumbers, bean sprouts contain the largest doses of silica. Bean sprouts like moong beans may be cooked, but are best eaten raw to reap full nutritional benefits. Toss the bean sprouts in a lunch salad and you may experience hair revival in a few months.

- ❖ **Biotin and protein**: Biotin deficiencies can result in brittle, damaged hair, while protein is regarded as the building block of hair. Eggs and legumes like kidney beans and lentils are packed with biotin and protein.

❖ **Zinc**: Nuts like walnuts, cashews, almonds, and pecans contain zinc, whose vitamin deficiency can lead to hair falling out. Add a handful of these nuts to your eating regimen as a healthy snack. Brazil nuts contain selenium, another nutrient important for hair growth. If you are a seafood lover, add oysters to your dinner plate next time you find yourself at the buffet.

❖ **B Vitamins**: Wholegrains store plentiful amounts of B vitamins that will deliver a kick of energy after you have hit the afternoon low. Eat breakfast cereal, wholewheat bread and short-grain brown rice, and you could see healthy, long hair in a few months' time.

Hair loss is a very common problem, and has easy solutions. More often than not, it isn't necessary to take expensive medication and use harsh shampoos and conditioners. Just maintaining a healthy diet, and using the home remedies will prove to be very helpful in the long run.

REMEDIES FOR HAIR LOSS

There are several natural home remedies, which are known to be effective in ensuring healthy and luscious hair. These can be used regularly to solve the ever-persistent problem of hair loss.

❖ Amla oil can be prepared at home by boiling 50 gm of dry amla pieces in 200 ml of coconut oil. Strain and store in a glass bottle. Apply on scalp once a week for increasing hair growth.

❖ Henna oil can also be prepared at home by boiling 50 gm of henna leaves in 200 ml of mustard oil. It is also helpful for hair growth and to reduce the dullness of hair.

❖ Once a week massage the scalp with a combination of coconut and almond oils to nourish the scalp.

❖ Add 1 tbsp lemon juice to 100 ml olive oil and massage the scalp with this to prevent dryness. Try this once a week.

❖ Apply a pack of coconut milk along with the white coconut flesh on the scalp once every fifteen days. It nourishes the scalp and prevents hair loss.

❖ Apply a pack of 100 gm of curd with 1 tsp of olive oil and 1 tsp of mint powder for shiny hair;

❖ Wash your hair with 50 gm of black gram powder and 10 gm of fenugreek powder in order to improve dry hair damaged by hair dyes, etc.

❖ Eat 5 almonds and 2 walnuts daily.

❖ Drink a juice made from 1 amla, 10 lettuce leaves, 10 mint leaves, ½ a beet, and 5 spinach leaves every morning. This strengthens the roots and prevents hair loss.

DANDRUFF

Dandruff is a common chronic scalp condition marked by itching and flaking of the skin on your scalp. Although dandruff isn't contagious and is rarely serious, it can be embarrassing and sometimes difficult to treat. But don't worry, help is here!

The good news is that dandruff can usually be controlled. Mild cases of dandruff may need nothing more than daily shampooing with a gentle cleanser. More stubborn cases of dandruff often respond to medicated shampoos.

For most teens and adults, dandruff symptoms are easy to spot: white, oily looking flakes of dead skin that dot your hair and shoulders, and an itchy, scaling scalp. The condition may worsen during the fall and winter, when indoor heating can contribute to dry skin, and improve during the summer.

What are the causes for dandruff to occur?

Dandruff can have several causes, including:

❖ **Dry skin**: Simple dry skin—the kind you get during winter when the air is cold and rooms are overheated—is the most common cause of itchy, flaking dandruff.

❖ **Irritated, oily skin**: This condition, one of the most frequent causes of dandruff, is marked by red, greasy skin covered with flaky white or yellow scales. This may affect other areas rich in oil glands, such as your eyebrows, the sides of your nose and the backs of your ears, your breastbone, your groin area, and sometimes your armpits.

❖ **Not shampooing often enough**: If you don't regularly wash your hair, oils and skin cells from your scalp can build up, causing dandruff.

❖ **Psoriasis**: This skin disorder causes an accumulation of dead skin cells that form thick, silvery scales. Psoriasis commonly occurs on your knees, elbows, and trunk, but it can also affect your scalp.

❖ **Eczema**: If you have eczema anywhere on your body, it could also be on your scalp, possibly leading to the development of dandruff.

❖ **Sensitivity to hair care products**: Sometimes sensitivities to certain ingredients in hair care products or hair dyes, especially paraphenylene diamine (PPD), can cause a red, itchy, scaling scalp. Shampooing too often or using too many styling products also may irritate your scalp, causing dandruff.

❖ **A yeast-like fungus (malassezia)**: Malassezia lives on the scalps of most healthy adults without causing problems. But sometimes it grows out of control, feeding on the oils secreted by your hair follicles. This can irritate the skin on your scalp and cause more skin cells to grow. The extra skin cells die and fall off, clumping with oil from your hair and scalp, making them appear white and flaky in your hair or on your clothes.

❖ **Poor diet**: If your diet lacks foods high in zinc, B vitamins, or certain types of fats, you may be more likely to have dandruff.

REMEDIES FOR DANDRUFF

Dandruff, though one of the most embarrassing hair problems, is fortunately easy to treat. So don't worry, follow these, and you will be able to wear that new black dress without a single worry!

❖ Soak 1 tbsp methi seeds in 100 ml water overnight. In the morning, add 1 tbsp apple cider vinegar and grind to a fine paste. Apply this paste to the scalp and keep for a few hours. Rinse off with cold water and use a mild shampoo to wash hair.

❖ Make a paste of 1 tbsp powdered melon seeds, 2 tbsp dahi, 1 tbsp lemon juice, and 1 tbsp honey. Apply on scalp and leave overnight. Rinse well and use a mild shampoo to wash hair.

❖ Another good pack to prevent dandruff is a mix of 2 tbsp moong powder, 4 tbsp dahi, and 1 tbsp olive oil. Let it stay on the scalp for a few hours and the rinse with cold water and wash with a mild shampoo.

Another easy way to prevent dandruff is to make camphorated marigold oil. You don't have to do a lot of fuss to make it, and trust me, it works! Follow this simple procedure to prepare it at home.

Ingredients

100 gm marigold flowers

500 ml coconut oil

A small piece of camphor

Preparation

- ❖ Boil 100 gm of marigold flowers in 500 ml coconut oil.
- ❖ Switch off the stove, add a small piece of camphor and cover with a lid.
- ❖ Let it cool completely, then strain and store in a dark glass bottle.
- ❖ Use once a week for healthy hair.

OILY HAIR

Oily, greasy hair—a sure sign that your tresses are in distress. Your greasy hair might just be screaming for help, and you fail to notice. The problem with oily hair is that many people don't understand the situation correctly. Washing the hair more frequently is the answer for 90 percent of oily hair sufferers. But what is really behind the problem and what steps can be taken to solve it permanently?

Oily hair is only the effect of having an oily scalp skin. You know that you can handle bad hair days, but oily hair days are a definite no. Although the cause of oily hair and skin is usually of genetic origin, there can be a number of factors that influence the production of excess sebum.

Excess oil on the scalp skin can lead to having very greasy

hair that needs constant washing. This leads to a vicious circle and it makes the problem worse in time.

What causes oily hair?

* **Genetic predisposition**: The skin can be genetically predisposed to produce more sebum than it normally should. Although there is not much you can do to change your genetic makeup, this condition can be cured using different types of natural remedies along with medication.
* **Hormonal imbalances create oily skin and hair**: When glands produce an overload of androgen hormones, you end up with oily hair and skin conditions. Moreover, disorders like polycystic ovaries syndrome (PCOS) in women can produce more sebum than required, which leads to oily hair and other related problems. When finding the main causes of oily hair and skin, a hormonal test should be taken to exclude hormonal imbalances.
* **Diet and hair, a link that should not be ignored**: Your hair is made of keratin, a protein that is also present in fingernails, and around 12 percent of hair is water. That's why hydration and diet are essential for healthy hair. Vitamin E, which is actually a part of sebum, is quite essential for hair, along with Vitamin B complex and iron.
* **Seborrhoeic dermatitis, a disease that can cause oily scalp and hair**: Dermatitis is a more severe skin condition that can be caused by overactive sebaceous glands along with a yeast infection of the skin. This condition can be worsened by a wide number of factors, such as diet, skin

lotions and shampoos, obesity, stress and anxiety, acne, and weather changes. Symptoms consist of oily skin and hair, flaking and itching of the scalp skin, hair loss, and redness on extensive areas of the skin.

❖ **Medication and oily hair**: Although sometimes doctors prescribe oral contraceptive pills to teenagers for certain hormonal dysfunctions, these can lead to other health problems, including oily skin and hair. Other types of pills, like steroids, can also bring about greasy hair and even hair loss.

❖ **Stress and anxiety can have a negative impact on your hair:** Anxiety can be a giant factor when it comes to health in general and sadly, hair is not immune to stress either. When you are stressed out your hair doesn't have its shine and will be greasy and sticky.

REMEDY FOR OILY HAIR

Even though oily hair can be a big pain, and you're sure it makes you look sick, there are ways to beat it.

❖ Make a hair pack of 2 egg yolks, 2 tbsp honey, 1 tsp corn flour, and 2 tsp rose water. Keep for an hour and rinse four-five times with cold water. Use a mild shampoo to wash hair.

❖ Make a paste of 4 tbsp baking soda and 1 tsp cornflour in 4-5 tbsp water. Wash your scalp with this, do not use shampoo. Then mix 2 tbsp white vinegar or apple cider or

---

6 tbsp lime juice in 1.5 litres of water. Use this to rinse off the pack.

❖ Take 2 sachets of green tea and 5 mint leaves and boil in 500 ml water. Leave aside to infuse further for half an hour. Add the juice of 1 lemon, strain and cool. Use this to rinse hair to reduce/prevent scalp/hair oiliness.

PREMATURE GREYING OF HAIR

Why do some people go grey in their twenties while others don't see the first sign of it until age 50?

Hair goes grey when colour-producing cells stop producing. Naturally occurring hydrogen peroxide can also build up in the hair, bleaching hair of its colour. Going grey by itself does not imply you have a medical problem, except in rare cases. Also, a Vitamin B-12 deficiency or difficulties with your pituitary or thyroid gland can cause premature greying that's reversible if the problem is corrected.

What causes premature greying?

❖ **Nutrition deficiency**: Improper intake of nutrients in the diet is one of the primary causes of premature greying of hair. Lack of Vitamins B, iron, copper, and iodine in the daily diet are believed to be a contributing factor.

❖ **Stress**: Prolonged period of stress and anxiety can have an adverse effect on the skin of the scalp, which interferes with the supply of vital nutrition necessary for the health of the hair.

❖ **Heredity**: It is one factor for premature greying.

❖ **Medical conditions**: Certain medical conditions, like thyroid imbalance, vitiligo, Vitamin B-12 deficiency, anaemia, etc., are said to be causes of premature greying.

❖ **Excessive heating of hair**: Washing hair with hot water and blow drying or straightening it has adverse effects on the hair.

❖ **Unclean scalp**: An unclean scalp weakens the root of the hair as dirt or oils get accumulated in the scalp. It prevents adequate blood supply to the hair shaft through the root to cause premature greying.

How can you prevent premature greying?

There is little you can do to control premature greying if it is a genetic issue. Although there is no cure for this disorder, you can take some preventive measures to prevent premature greying, such as:

❖ Diet plays a major role in preventing and arresting premature greying of hair. So, eat foods rich in pantothenic acid (Vitamin B-5). These include mushrooms, oat and wheat bran, sunflower seeds, liver, fish, and avocadoes.

❖ Proper grooming of hair is essential to maintain a healthy hair texture and strong roots.

- ❖ Use shampoo and conditioners which are mild and suit your hair type.
- ❖ Avoid hot water to wash your hair.
- ❖ Massage the scalp with your fingertips to ensure proper blood circulation within the scalp.
- ❖ Avoid smoking.

REMEDY TO PREVENT PREMATURE GREYING

Here is the recipe for an oil, which if used once a week can prevent premature greying of hair.

Ingredients

20 curry leaves
1 chopped amla
5 guava leaves
200 ml pure coconut oil

Preparation

- ❖ Take the curry leaves, chopped amla and guava leaves, and boil them in 200 ml pure coconut oil.
- ❖ Let them turn black in the oil and then switch of the stove.
- ❖ Cover and let it cool.
- ❖ Pass the oil through a muslin cloth and store in a dark-coloured bottle.
- ❖ Now this oil is ready to use!

DRY HAIR

Do you dream of having the luxurious, silky hair? Understanding the root cause of dry hair and taking the necessary action may be all you need to get the locks you long for.

What are the common causes?

Your hair can get dry because your scalp doesn't make enough oil to moisturize your hair, or your hair lets moisture escape. Some common causes of dry hair include:

❖ **Excessive washing and blow-drying, harsh shampoos**: Avoid harsh shampoos completely and definitely stop washing your hair every day. Also, protect your hair from the heat of blow dryers and curling irons. Start washing your hair twice or thrice a week with a very mild shampoo and conditioner.

❖ **Environmental dryness**: If you live in an area with excessive sun, dry heat, and little to no humidity you will have much drier hair than someone who lives in a tropical, humid climate. A way to reduce this damage is by wearing a hat in the sun and never forgetting the swimming cap in a chlorinated pool.

❖ **Anorexia**: Because people with anorexia engage in self-starving to stay dangerously thin, their bodies are denied the nutrients they need to function. This includes the nutrients necessary to maintain lustre, shine, and softness in their hair. Dry hair (along with dry skin and hair loss) is a common side effect of anorexia, and one that may manifest early on.

- **Malnutrition:** A person who is malnourished does not take in the nutrients necessary for the body to maintain healthy hair. As a result, the hair becomes dry, brittle, and damaged. In particular, dry hair can be a sign that your diet is lacking in Omega-3 essential fatty acids, which can be found in salmon and fish oil, walnuts, and flaxseeds.
- **Hypothyroidism:** In this condition, the body produces very little thyroid hormone and dry, brittle, and thin hair is one of the earliest symptoms of this disease. Other symptoms include weakness, fatigue, depression, and joint or muscle pain. This disease causes the body to become sluggish in its functions, which leads to unfit mental and physical conditions along with some other mild to severe symptoms.

REMEDIES FOR DRY HAIR

Now, after reading the causes itself, I'm sure you understand that treating dry hair is all about taking the correct treatment as well as eating right. Apart from that, here are some quick home remedies that you can follow to get beautiful hair:

- Gently warm 1 tbsp each of coconut oil, sesame oil, olive oil, and almond oil. Add 5 strands of kesar and let it infuse for 10 minutes. Massage this warm mixture on to dry hair while avoiding the scalp. Wrap your hair in a towel and leave on for 30 minutes. Use a diluted shampoo to wash off.

❖ Take 1 well-beaten egg yolk, 2 egg whites, and 1 tbsp sunflower oil and use this as a hair mask. After applying, leave on for 30 minutes. Use a shower cap. Wash hair using a mild shampoo and lukewarm or cold water. Be careful not to use hot water or else the egg will cook on your scalp!

❖ Eat 2 walnuts or 1 tbsp flaxseed or 1 avocado daily.

Hair and skin are an essential part of our appearance. They matter to us not just because of what people think of us, but also because of what we think of ourselves. I hope this chapter on skin and hair issues has given you more insight about how to deal with these minor and yet important matters. Like I always say, good health always!

PART 3

USING HERBS TO PREVENT AND CURE MAJOR ILLNESSES

9

Heart Issues

WHAT ARE WE WITHOUT THE HEART?

It is the centre of all bodily functions, and is the organ that keeps us going every day without skipping a beat. The requirements of the heart are like all other muscles: oxygen and nutrient-rich blood to function. The coronary arteries that provide blood to the heart muscle extend across the surface of the heart, starting at the base of the aorta and branching out to every area of the heart muscle.

However, the coronary arteries are at risk of narrowing as cholesterol deposits, called plaques, build up inside the artery. If the arteries become narrow enough, blood supply to the heart muscle may slow down, and this sluggish blood flow to the heart causes pain, or angina.

We have to give our heart special care. However, in the stressed and hectic days that we live in most of us forget the most important organ that keeps us going. Risk factors for heart disease include smoking, high BP, high cholesterol, diabetes, family history of heart malfunction, peripheral artery disease, and obesity.

CORONARY ARTERY DISEASE

What are the symptoms of heart disease?

Coronary artery disease is symptomized by chest pain associated with shortness of breath. The pain of angina can be described as a pressure or heaviness behind the breastbone with radiation to the jaw and down the arm accompanied by shortness of breath and sweating. Unfortunately for patients, angina has a variety of signs and symptoms, and often, there may not even be any specific chest pain. Other symptoms may include shoulder or back ache, upper abdominal pain, nausea, and indigestion.

People with coronary artery disease usually have a gradual progression of their symptoms. As an artery narrows over time, the symptoms of decreased blood flow to part of the heart muscle may increase in frequency and/or severity. Doctors may inquire about changes in exercise tolerance (How far can you walk before getting symptoms? Is it to the nearest bus stop? Up a flight of stairs?), and whether there has been an acute change in the symptoms.

Once again, patients may be asymptomatic until a heart attack occurs. Of course, some patients also may be in denial as to their symptoms and procrastinate in seeking care.

All the various types of heart diseases require different treatments but share similar warning signs. It is imperative that you consult your doctor for the correct diagnosis and prompt treatment. You should learn to recognize the symptoms of heart disease and call your doctor the moment you begin to experience them.

CONSULT YOUR DOCTOR IF YOU'RE FEELING ANY OF THESE SYMPTOMS

❖ Chest pain
❖ Pain in the shoulders, arms, neck, throat, jaw, or back too
❖ Shortness of breath
❖ Palpitations (irregular heartbeats, or a 'flip-flop' feeling in your chest)
❖ A faster heartbeat
❖ Weakness or dizziness

HEART ATTACKS

During a heart attack, symptoms characteristically last 30 minutes or longer and are not relieved by rest or oral medications. Initial symptoms may start as a mild discomfort that progresses to significant pain.

Some people have a heart attack without having any symptoms, which is known as a 'silent' myocardial infarction (MI). It is important to remember that this occurs more often in people with diabetes.

Symptoms of a heart attack

❖ discomfort, pressure, heaviness, or pain in the chest, arm, or below the breastbone
❖ discomfort radiating to the back, jaw, throat, or arm
❖ fullness, indigestion, or choking feeling (may feel like heartburn)
❖ sweating, nausea, vomiting, or dizziness
❖ extreme weakness, anxiety, or shortness of breath
❖ rapid or irregular heartbeats

OTHER HEART DISEASES

The heart, if not cared for, can malfunction in other ways too. Some of it may be genetic, and a family history of heart disease is the first indicator that you should get yourself checked immediately by your doctor. I've listed few (from the numerous heart issues that may arise).

Symptoms of arrhythmias

Symptoms of arrhythmias, or an abnormal heart rhythm, include:
❖ palpitations (a feeling of skipped heartbeats, fluttering or flip-flops in your chest)
❖ pounding in chest
❖ dizziness or feeling light-headed
❖ fainting
❖ shortness of breath

- ❖ chest discomfort
- ❖ weakness or fatigue (feeling very tired)

Symptoms of atrial fibrillation

Atrial fibrillation (AF) is a type of arrhythmiaand most people with AF experience one or more of these symptoms:
- ❖ heart palpitations (a sudden pounding, fluttering, or racing feeling in the heart)
- ❖ lack of energy
- ❖ dizziness (feeling faint or light-headed).
- ❖ chest discomfort (pain, pressure, or discomfort in the chest)
- ❖ shortness of breath (difficulty breathing during normal activities)

Some patients with AF have no symptoms and these episodes are often brief.

Symptoms of heart valve disease

Symptoms of heart valve disease include:
- ❖ shortness of breath and/or difficulty catching breath. You will notice this most when you are doing your daily activities or when you are lying down flat on the bed.
- ❖ weakness or dizziness
- ❖ discomfort in your chest. You may feel a weight in your chest with movement or when going out in cold air
- ❖ palpitations (rapid heart rhythm, irregular heartbeat, skipped beats, or a flip-flop feeling in your chest)

If valve disease causes heart failure, symptoms may include:
* Swelling of your ankles or feet. Swelling may also arise in your abdomen, which may result in you feeling bloated
* Quick weight gain (a weight gain of two or three kilos in one day is probable)

Symptoms of heart valve disease do not always transmit the seriousness of your condition. You may have no symptoms and have severe valve disease, requiring timely treatment. Or, in contrast, as with mitral valve prolapse, you may have severe symptoms, yet tests may illustrate minor valve disease.

Symptoms of heart failure

Symptoms of heart failure can include:
* shortness of breath noted during activity (most commonly) or at rest, especially when you lie down flat in bed
* cough that creates a white sputum
* rapid weight gain (a weight gain of two or three kilos in one day is probable)
* swelling in ankles, legs, and abdomen
* dizziness
* fatigue and weakness
* rapid or irregular heartbeats
* other symptoms include nausea, palpitations, and chest pain

Like with valve disease, heart failure symptoms may not be connected to how weak your heart is. You may have numerous symptoms, but your heart function may be only mildly weakened. On the other hand you may have a severely damaged heart, with hardly any symptoms.

Symptoms of congenital heart defects

Congenital heart defects maybe diagnosed before birth, right after birth, during childhood, or not until adulthood also. It is actually possible to have a defect and no signs at all. Sometimes it can be identified because of a heart murmur on a physical examination, an abnormal EKG, or a chest X-ray in a person with no symptoms.

In adults, if symptoms of congenital heart disease are there, they will consist of:
❖ shortness of breath
❖ limited ability to exercise
❖ symptoms of heart failure (see above) or valve disease (see above)

Symptoms of heart muscle disease

Countless people with heart muscle disease, or cardiomyopathy, have no symptoms or only small symptoms, and live an ordinary life. In contrast, other people develop symptoms, which grow and worsen as heart function worsens.

Symptoms of cardiomyopathy may occur at any age and may include:
❖ chest pain or pressure (occurs usually with exercise or physical activity, but can also take place with rest or following meals)

- ❖ heart failure symptoms (see above)
- ❖ swelling of the lower extremities
- ❖ fatigue.
- ❖ fainting
- ❖ palpitations (fluttering in the chest due to abnormal heart rhythms)

Some people also have arrhythmias. These lead to sudden death in a minute number of people with cardiomyopathy.

Symptoms of pericarditis

When present, symptoms of pericarditis may include:
- ❖ chest pain: This pain is dissimilar from angina. It is sharp and situated in the centre of the chest. The main difference is that the pain radiates to the neck and sporadically, the arms and back. Remember that, it is worsened when lying down, taking a deep breath in, coughing, or swallowing, and relieved when you sit forward.
- ❖ low-grade fever
- ❖ increased heart rate

How is Heart Disease Diagnosed?

The first step towards diagnosis is finding out if potential for heart disease exists in patient history. The recommended testing depends on the fact that patient actually shows angina and the potential of heart disease that he may have.
- ❖ catheterization

❖ electrocardiogram (ECG or EKG)
❖ stress testing
❖ echocardiography
❖ perfusion studies
❖ computerized tomography

Prevention: What You Can Do

First and foremost: Live a healthy lifestyle

Eat a healthy diet
Choosing healthy meal and snack options can help you avoid heart disease and its complications. Be sure to eat plenty of fresh fruits and vegetables. Eating foods low in saturated fat and cholesterol and high in fibre can help prevent high blood cholesterol. Limiting salt or sodium in your diet can also lower your blood pressure.

Maintain a healthy weight
Being overweight or obese can increase your risk for heart disease. To determine whether your weight is in a healthy range, doctors often calculate the BMI. Doctors sometimes also use waist and hip measurements to measure a person's excess body fat.

Exercise regularly
Physical activity can help you maintain a healthy weight and lower cholesterol and blood pressure. The Surgeon General of the US, the nations leading spokesman on matters of public health,

recommends that adults should engage in moderate-intensity exercise for at least 30 minutes on most days of the week.

Don't smoke
Cigarette smoking greatly increases your risk for heart disease. So, if you don't smoke, don't start. If you do smoke, quitting will lower your risk for heart disease.

Limit alcohol use
Avoid drinking too much alcohol because it causes high blood pressure.

Prevent or treat your other medical conditions

If you have high cholesterol, high blood pressure, or diabetes, there are steps you can take to lower your risk for heart disease.

❖ **Have your cholesterol checked**: You should test your cholesterol levels at least once every five years.

❖ **Monitor your blood pressure**: High blood pressure has no symptoms, so be sure to have it checked on a regular basis.

❖ **Manage your diabetes**: If you have diabetes, closely monitor your blood sugar levels.

❖ **Take your medicine**: If you're taking medication to treat high cholesterol, high blood pressure, or diabetes, follow your doctor's instructions carefully.

What is a heart-healthy diet?

Changing your eating habits can be tough. Start with these eight strategies to work your way towards a heart healthy.

Although you might know that eating certain foods can increase your heart disease risk, it's often tough to change your eating habits. Once you know which foods to eat more of and which foods to limit, you'll be on your way toward a heart healthy.

1) Control your portion size

How much you eat is just as important as what you eat. Overloading your plate, taking seconds and eating until you feel stuffed can lead to eating more calories, fat and cholesterol than you should.

Keep track of the number of servings you eat—and use proper serving sizes—to help control your portions.

2) Eat more vegetables and fruits

Vegetables and fruits are good sources of vitamins and minerals. They are also low in calories and rich in dietary fibre. Eating more fruits and vegetables will help you eat less high-fat foods, such as meat, cheese, and junk food.

Keep vegetables washed and cut in your refrigerator for quick snacks. Choose recipes that have vegetables or fruits as the main ingredient, such as vegetable stir fry or fresh fruit mixed into salads.

Fruits and vegetables to choose	Fruits and vegetables to avoid
• Fresh or frozen vegetables and fruits • Low-sodium canned vegetables • Canned fruit packed in juice or water	• Coconut as well as tender coconut meal (malai) • Vegetables with creamy sauces • Fried or breaded vegetables • Canned fruit packed in heavy syrup • Frozen fruit with sugar added

Note: However, please remember that a glass of coconut water should be consumed for the high potassium content.

3) Wholegrains

Wholegrains are good sources of fibre and other nutrients that play a role in regulating blood pressure and heart health. Be adventurous and try a new wholegrain, such as couscous, quinoa, or barley.

Another easy way to add wholegrains to your diet is ground flaxseed. They can lower your total blood cholesterol. You can grind the seeds and stir a teaspoon of them into your food.

Grain products to choose	Grain products to limit or avoid
• Wholewheat flour • Wholegrain bread • High-fibre cereal with 5 gm or more of fibre in a serving	• White, refined flour • White bread (maida bread) and brown bread (it is generally coloured with caramel/ brown colour)

Grain products to choose	Grain products to limit or avoid
• Wholegrains such as brown rice, barley, and buckwheat (kasha/kuttu) • Wholegrain pasta • Oatmeal (steel cut or regular) • Ground flaxseed	• Muffins • Frozen waffles • Corn bread • Doughnuts • Biscuits • Granola bars • Cakes • Pies • Egg noodles • Buttered popcorn • High-fat snack crackers

4) Limit unhealthy fats and cholesterol

Limiting how much saturated and trans fats you eat is an important step to reduce your blood cholesterol and lower your risk of coronary artery disease.

REMEDY TO LOWER LDL

A combination of fenugreek seeds, dried fenugreek leaves, flaxseeds, chia seeds, dried mint powder, dried celery, and jeera will help with bringing down LDL cholesterol levels considerably.

The best way to reduce saturated and trans fats in your diet is to limit the amount of solid fats—butter, margarine and shortening—you add to food when cooking and serving. You can also reduce the amount of saturated fat in your diet by trimming fat off your meat or choosing lean meats with less than 10 percent fat.

Polyunsaturated fats, found in nuts and seeds, also are good choices for a heart healthy. When used in place of saturated fat, monounsaturated and polyunsaturated fats may help lower your total blood cholesterol. But moderation is essential. All types of fat are high in calories.

Fats to choose	Fats to limit
• Olive oil	• Butter
• Safflower oil	• Lard
• Sunflower oil	• Bacon fat
• Sesame oil	• Gravy
• Peanut oil	• Cream sauce
• Mustard oil	• Non-dairy creamers
• Rice bran oil	• Hydrogenated margarine and shortening
	• Cocoa butter, found in chocolate
	• Coconut, palm, cottonseed and palm-kernel oils

5) Choose low-fat protein sources

Lean meat, poultry, and fish, low-fat dairy products, and egg whites or egg substitutes are some of your best sources of protein. You'll find the highest amounts of Omega-3 fatty acids in cold-water fish, such as salmon, mackerel, and herring. Other sources are flaxseed, walnuts, soybeans, and canola oil.

Beans, peas, and lentils are also good sources of protein and contain less fat and no cholesterol, making them good substitutes for meat. Substituting plant protein for animal protein—for example, a soy or bean burger for a hamburger—will reduce your fat and cholesterol intake.

Proteins to choose	Proteins to limit or avoid
• Low-fat dairy products such as skim or low-fat (1 percent) milk, yoghurt, and cheese • Egg whites or egg substitutes • Fish such as salmon • Skinless poultry • Legumes • Soybeans and soy products, for example, soy burgers and tofu • Lean ground meats	• Full-fat milk and other dairy products • Organ meats, such as liver • Egg yolks • Fatty meats • Spare ribs • Cold cuts • Hot dogs and sausages • Bacon • Fried or breaded meats

6) Reduce the sodium in your food

Reducing sodium is an essential part of a heart healthy. It is recommended that:

❖ fit adults have no more than a teaspoon a day
❖ people aged 51 or older, people who have been detected with high BP, diabetes, or chronic kidney disease have no more than 1,500 mg of sodium a day.

But a good deal of the salt you consume comes from canned or processed foods, like soups and frozen dinners.

Eating fresh foods and cooking your own soups and stews can decrease the amount of salt you ingest. **Be distrustful of foods that say they are lower in sodium since they are seasoned with sea salt instead of regular table salt—sea salt actually has the identical nutritional value as regular salt.**

Low-salt items to choose	High-salt items to avoid
• Herbs and spices • Salt substitutes • You could also make a low salt butter at home by keeping a 100 gm slab of butter in a bowl of iced water overnight in the fridge	• Table salt • Canned soups and prepared foods, such as frozen dinners, ready-to-eat, and packaged meals • Tomato juice • Soy sauce

BE HEART HEALTHY

❖ Have 1 tbsp ground flax daily. If you are eating flaxseed, then ensure that you chew the seeds well. If you are eating flax seeds for their Omega 3 fatty acid content, then eat the food they are in within a few days because the oil will degrade. Eat as is or add to salads, dips, dressings, etc.

❖ Chia seeds also have heart-healthy benefits. Soak 1 tbsp of chia in water for 20 minutes, then consume as is or incorporate into smoothies/milkshakes/chaas.

❖ Snack on 2 to 3 walnuts, 1 tbsp of sunflower seeds/melon seeds/pumpkin seeds, 6 to 7 unsalted pistachios, and 1 fig in the evening.

10

Blood Pressure

RITA WAS 26 YEARS OLD AND UNDERWEIGHT WHEN SHE CAME to me with a problem: she used to be dizzy all the time, and would feel extremely tired and listless for a woman her age. Her mother-in-law thought that she was just being lazy and shirking her kitchen duties. When I asked for her dietary recall, she told me that she used to have a glass of doodhi juice every morning.

Doodhi juice is good for alleviating high blood pressure (BP) but disastrous for someone with low BP. Her symptoms pointed at low BP to me, so I checked her BP. I was appalled to see that her BP was 78/53. No wonder she was so listless, she couldn't even concentrate on our conversation. I asked her to stop taking the juice immediately and then record her BP every morning for a week. Her BP was still very low (below 100/60). I then asked her to start drinking a minimum of three glasses of buttermilk with salt and jeera, as well as two glasses of nimbu paani with both salt and sugar. Gradually, her BP increased and she stopped getting those dizzy spells and blackouts. Today, her BP is at a healthy 110/75, and she is now the perfect bahu.

The important question that you must be asking yourself is why is high or low blood pressure is such a big deal? Why does the doctor check your BP each time you visit him.

BP is the measure of the force of blood pushing against blood vessel walls. The heart pumps blood into the arteries (blood vessels), which carry the blood throughout the body. High BP, also called hypertension, is dangerous because it makes the heart work harder to pump blood to the body and contributes to hardening of the arteries, or atherosclerosis, and to the development of heart failure.

Uncomplicated high BP usually occurs without any symptoms (silently) and so hypertension has been labelled the 'silent killer'. It is called this because the disease can progress to finally develop any one or more of the several potentially fatal complications such as heart attacks or strokes. Uncomplicated hypertension may be present and remain unnoticed for many years, or even decades. This happens because there are no symptoms, and those affected fail to undergo periodic BP screening. Some people with uncomplicated hypertension, however, may experience symptoms such as headache, dizziness, shortness of breath, and blurred vision usually when BP is very high.

WHAT ARE THE CAUSES OF HIGH BP?

The exact causes of high BP are not known, but several factors and conditions may play a role in its development, including:

* ❖ smoking
* ❖ being overweight or obese
* ❖ lack of physical activity
* ❖ too much salt in the diet
* ❖ too much alcohol consumption (more than 1 to 2 drinks per day)
* ❖ stress
* ❖ old age
* ❖ family history of high blood pressure
* ❖ chronic kidney disease
* ❖ adrenal and thyroid disorders

Fifty-two-year-old Rajeev was extremely agitated when he first met me. Despite doing everything that his doctor ordered, including taking his BP medications regularly, his BP still kept rising and his doctor wanted to increase his medication. His BP used to fluctuate between 150/104 and 145/99. Rajeev was already on a low-salt diet and had given up most of his favourite foods because of their high sodium content. His work pressure had increased tremendously in the last couple of months, and he was worried about his BP as he didn't foresee a change in the stress level at work in the near future. He wanted a quick fix to show improvement in his BP just so that he would not have to take anymore medication. I asked him to give me three months to help him maintain normal BP.

I initially asked him to have a glass of green juice every morning, which included a big bunch of fresh coriander, 25 mint leaves, 2 sprigs of parsley, 2 stalks of celery, and 1 tbsp of lemon juice. This had to be diluted with water to make up one glass and had to be consumed on rising.

Apart from this, he was also asked to drink 3 litres of therapeutic water between 10 am and 7 pm. His therapeutic water had 4 stalks of fresh celery, a 2-inch piece of cinnamon, 10 basil leaves, and half a lemon (including the rind). He was requested to finish the water by 7 pm as it was a diuretic and I didn't want him to spend half the night in the washroom!

Within a month, his BP had normalized, but his doctor was skeptical about decreasing his medication. So Rajeev continued allopathic medication along with naturopathy for another month. Now his BP started falling below normal levels.

His doctor very reluctantly agreed to lower his medication but cautioned him about stopping it altogether. Rajeev was very happy that much before the three-month stipulation he had been able to bring his BP under control. Currently, he's on a minimal dosage of allopathic medication, simply because his doctor has threatened him that he won't see him anymore if he stops. I am still working on helping him stop his BP medication completely. However, he is extremely satisfied that not only does he not have to take extra medication that his doctor was suggesting initially, but his previous medication has also been reduced! He has shown his appreciation by recommending most of his highly stressed colleagues to me!

CONTROLLING BP ISSUES

You must understand that more than anything, herbs and spices play a vital role in the treatment of high or low blood pressure. I'll give you a few tips and remedies for both high and low BP.

REMEDIES TO IMPROVE LOW BP

❖ A glass of water with a pinch a pepper powder, 1 tbsp lime juice, ½ tsp salt, and 1 tsp of honey taken every morning on rising will help to keep the blood pressure from falling. Half an hour later have a glass of spinach and beetroot juice.

❖ Avoid juices with white pumpkin and celery because they will further decrease the blood pressure.

❖ Make a mix of flax meal, dried celery, dried parsley, fennel, cinnamon, and cumin, and eat 1 tsp of this mix thrice a day.

❖ Drink a minimum of 1.5 litres of celery-infused water between mid-morning and 7 pm. To make celery-infused water, simply add 2 stalks of fresh celery to a bottle of water and drink through the day. Be careful not to drink large amounts of this water at one go because it will reduce your blood pressure quickly and cause dizziness.

FOODS THAT CONTROL HIGH BP

While blood pressure is mostly unavoidable, you can help reduce higher BP by incorporating the following eating habits in your lifestyle:

❖ Avoid salty foods and snacks including processed meats (bacon, salami, ham) wafers, packaged soups, sauces, and pickles;

❖ Eat foods rich in potassium, like bananas, water melon, celery, parsley, mint, and coriander;

❖ Eat seeds like pumpkin seeds, melon seeds, cucumber seeds, flaxseeds.

11

Diabetes

INDIA IS RANKED ONLY AFTER CHINA IN TERMS OF THE NUMBER of people diagnosed with diabetes. According to the International Diabetes Federation, as of 2011, 61.5 million Indians are diagnosed with diabetes. The rampancy of this disease is alarming, and we need to take steps for prevention. The first step towards this is to arm ourselves with the knowledge of the disease, and regulate our diet. Diabetes (*diabetes mellitus*) is one of the most problematic diseases of today.

It is classed as a metabolism disorder. Metabolism refers to the way our bodies use digested food for energy and growth. Most of what we eat is broken down into glucose. Glucose is the principal source of fuel for our bodies. When our food is digested, the glucose makes its way into our bloodstream. Our cells use the glucose for energy and growth. However, glucose cannot enter our cells without insulin being present—insulin makes it possible for our cells to take in the glucose.

Insulin is a hormone that is produced by the pancreas. After eating, the pancreas automatically release an adequate quantity of insulin to move the glucose present in our blood into the cells, as soon as glucose enters the cells blood glucose levels drop.

A person with diabetes has a condition in which the quantity of glucose in the blood is too elevated (hyperglycemia). This happens because the body does not produce enough or no insulin, or has cells that do not respond properly to the insulin the pancreas produces. This results in too much glucose building up in the blood. The excess blood glucose eventually passes out of the body in urine. So, even though the blood has plenty of glucose, the cells are not receiving it for their essential energy and growth requirements.

Diabetes in Greek means a 'siphon'. In 1675, Thomas Willis added 'mellitus' to the term. Mel in Latin means 'honey'; the urine and blood of people with diabetes has excess glucose, and glucose is sweet like honey. Diabetes mellitus could literally mean 'siphoning off sweet water'.

There are three types of diabetes:

Type 1 Diabetes

Also known as insulin dependent, juvenile, or early onset diabetes. In Type 1 diabetes, the body doesn't produce insulin.

It is less common as compared to Type 2 diabetes, with approximately 10 percent of all diabetes cases being Type 1. Patients suffering from Type 1 diabetes have to take insulin injections for the rest of their lives and also need to ensure balanced blood glucose levels by conducting regular blood tests and eating a special diet.

A person with Type 1 will have to watch what he eats. Foods that are low in fat, salt, and have no or very little added sugar are ideal. He should consume foods that have complex carbohydrates, rather than fast carbohydrates, as well as fruits and vegetables. **A diet that controls the person's blood sugar level as well as his BP and cholesterol levels will help achieve the best possible results.**

Devendra Patel, a man suffering from Type 1 diabetes for the past 30 years, was introduced to me by his wife, Parvati, and daughter-in-law, Radha, both of whom I was already helping. He had the scepticism and irritation of a long-time diabetic, and was extremely reluctant to allow any change in his diet. He claimed to know everything about his own condition, but surprisingly never even checked his blood sugar—pre- or post-meal. Rather, he would ask the cook what was prepared for lunch or dinner and adjust his insulin dosage accordingly.

In my first session with him, the entire family sat with him and me, and talked about his eating habits. Maybe because he was browbeaten into it, or maybe because he wanted to, Devendra agreed to take the mix (which included flax, dried basil, methi, jeera, dried parsley, white sesame seeds, cinnamon powder, gudmar, fennel seeds and onion seeds). I gave him a diet plan, which he regulated according to what was made.

at home. As it so happened, the family went on a holiday to New York, and being a man with an incorrigible sweet tooth, he wanted to indulge himself. Indulgence is a good thing, as long as it isn't a habit and that's what I told him. He enjoyed the holiday, and the cheesecake and took a slightly increased dosage of the prescribed mix.

Two months later, his endocrinologist had reduced his insulin dosage by 6 units and had promised to put him on a minimal dosage of 2 units if he continued to show a decrease in his blood sugar for the next six months. Three months later, he showed me the reduced readings and grinning sheepishly, shook hands, and said that maybe he didn't know after all!

His case is important to me also because it reinforced the importance of going to someone's house and consulting. If it hadn't been the insistence of his family in those family sessions, Devendra probably would have never realized the error of his ways.

TYPE 2 DIABETES

Type 2 diabetes is mostly developed in people who are overweight, and remains to be the most common form of diabetes. It also occurs later in life, if compared with Type 1 diabetes.

A person with Type 2 diabetes either:
❖ does not produce enough insulin or
❖ suffers from 'insulin resistance'

In the case of insulin resistance, the body produces insulin, but insulin sensitivity is reduced and it does not do the job as well as it should. Glucose does not enter the body's cells properly, causing two problems:

❖ a build-up of glucose in the blood
❖ the cells are not receiving the glucose they need for energy and growth

In the early stages of Type 2 diabetes, insulin sensitivity is the main abnormality—also there are elevated levels of insulin in the blood. There are medications which can improve insulin sensitivity and reduce glucose production by the liver.

It is not uncommon for people to achieve long-term satisfactory glucose control by doing more exercise, bringing down their body weight, and cutting down on their dietary intake of carbohydrates.

However, despite these measures, the tendency towards insulin resistance will continue, so the patient must persist with his increased physical activity, monitored diet, and body weight. As a person with Type 2 does produce his own insulin, a combination of oral medicines will usually improve insulin production, regulate the release of glucose by the liver, and treat insulin resistance to some extent.

Ajinkya Majumdar a 48-year-old man diagnosed with Type 2 diabetes 12 years ago. His work stress was so high and combined with sleep apnea and high blood pressure, he had a very difficult time coping with it all. His lifestyle gave him no time to exercise and his eating habits were also very erratic. His wife, Niharika, barely got any sleep because of his snoring.

When I first met him, Ajinkya's BP was 164/89, his fasting blood sugar (FBS) was 189, post-prandial blood sugar (PPBS) was 264, and the glycosylated haemoglobin level (HbA1c) was 8.9. Such high levels were a cause for concern, and his wife also remained very troubled and worried a lot.

I first gave him a detox mix (which included flax, mint, dried celery, cinnamon, jeera, and green elaichi), put him on 1,600-calorie diabetic diet and asked him to walk for about 35 minutes, four days a week. Within three weeks, his FBS had come down to 145 and PPBS to 203. Subsequently, gudmar and fenugreek seeds were added to his mix.

The next time I met him, his BP had reduced to 137/81 and his FBS to 128, but his PPBS still remained 200. In an attempt to find out what was going wrong, he was asked to recall what he ate. As it turns out, Niharika had stopped packing mithai in his lunch dabba, and Ajinkya had taken to eating a lump of jaggery immediately after lunch! I advised him to eat a date the next time he had a sugar craving and within a week's time, his PPBS also came down to 183.

After three months he reported that his BP was 132/79, FBS 99, PPBS 153, and Hb1Ac was 7.1. Niharika called to say that she was sleeping soundly for the first time in years, since her husband's snoring had become that minimal.

Diabetes can be controlled with the proper diet and exercise routine—an invaluable lesson to be learnt!

GESTATIONAL DIABETES

This type of diabetes affects women during pregnancy. Some women have very high levels of glucose in their blood, and their bodies are unable to produce enough insulin to transport all of the glucose into their cells, resulting in progressively rising levels of glucose. Diagnosis of gestational diabetes is made during pregnancy. Gestational diabetics can very often control their diabetes with exercise and diet itself.

Between 10 to 20 percent of women will need to take some kind of blood-glucose-controlling medications. Undiagnosed or uncontrolled gestational diabetes can raise the risk of complications during childbirth. The baby may be bigger than he should be because of the increase in sugar levels of the amniotic fluid.

Tara and Nelson Gill had been married for 11 years, when Tara conceived for the first time. She was very anxious about the growth of the foetus and every time she went for an ultrasound, she went prepared to hear bad news. Tara had gestational diabetes, hypothyroidism, and oedema.

When I first met her, she was in the fifth month of her pregnancy and was taking medication for diabetes and hypothyroidism. Both her gynaecologist and endocrinologist had warned her against gaining more than 9 kg totally throughout her gestation period and she had already put on 7 kg in the first five months itself.

Tara's condition was deteriorating rapidly. Her BP was fairly high, her FBS was 76, but PPBS 289 and her Thyroid Stimulating Hormone (TSH) levels were at 11.7. The oedema around her ankles made walking very painful and that combined with the water retention, combined to her weight gain significantly.

Her mix (which included flax, cinnamon, dried curry leaves, bay leaves, jeera, saunf, and fenugreek seeds) didn't include gudmar as I did not recommend it because of her hypothyroidism. I also advised her to put two stalks of celery in 2 litres of water and drink from morning to 7 pm. Within a week she reported a decrease in oedema and after three weeks, her PPBS was down to 212, and TSH reduced to 9. Her relief was palpable and she was extremely happy as she was eating healthy foods, had no craving for savoury snacks, and most importantly, had not gained any weight in that three-week period.

A month later, she had gained a meagre 650 gm, her FBS was 79, PPBS, 147, and the TSH levels were down to 7.3. Her prescribed mix now also included kasoori methi and coriander seeds. She no longer needed celery in her water, but was advised to add ½ tsp ajwain to two litres of water to help her with digestion.

By the time she was due for delivery, she had gained a total of 12.2 kg, her FBS was 72, PPBS was 130, and TSH levels were at 5.5. Baby Urvi came into this world at 39 weeks of gestation, and weighed a healthy nine pounds. Her parents dote on her, and she is the light of their lives.

What you need to know about diabetes and diet

Eating right is vital if you're trying to prevent or control diabetes. While exercise is also important, what you eat has the biggest impact when it comes to weight loss.

But what does eating right for diabetes mean?

You may be surprised to hear that your nutritional needs are virtually the same for everyone else: no special foods or complicated diets are necessary.

A diabetes diet is simply a healthy eating plan that is high in nutrients, low in fat, and moderate in calories. It is a healthy diet for anyone! The only difference is that you need to pay more attention to some of your food choices—most notably the carbohydrates you eat.

Diabetes and diet tip 1: Choose high-fibre, slow-release carbs

Carbohydrates have a big impact on your blood-sugar levels—more so than fats and proteins—but you don't have to avoid them. You just need to be smart about what types of carbs you eat.

In general, it's best to limit highly refined carbohydrates like white bread, pasta, and rice, as well as soda, candy, and snack foods. Focus instead on high-fibre complex carbohydrates—also known as slow-release carbs. Slow-release carbs help keep blood-sugar levels even because they are digested more slowly, thus preventing your body from producing too much insulin. They also provide lasting energy and help you stay full longer.

Choosing carbs that are packed with fibre (and don't spike your blood sugar)	
Instead of…	Try these high-fibre options…
White rice	Brown rice/quinoa/kamut/spelt
White potatoes (including fries and mashed potatoes)	Sweet potatoes, yams, tapioca, cauliflower mash
Regular pasta	Wholewheat pasta
White bread	Wholewheat or wholegrain bread
Sugary breakfast cereal	High-fibre breakfast cereal (raisin bran, etc.) Kamut flakes Spelt flakes
Instant oatmeal	Steel-cut oats or rolled oats (slow cooked)
Croissant or pastry	Bran muffin
Paratha	Whole wheat/multi grain rotis
Uttapam	Oatmeal uttapam
Idlis	Rava idlis
Humus chickpeas	Seed humus (sunflower/pumpkin/melon seed)

Making the glycemic index (GI) easy

What foods are slow release foods? Several tools have been designed to help answer this question. The GI is a numerical system of measurement that tells you how quickly a food turns into sugar in your system. Glucose has a GI of 100 and hence the GI gives each food a rating between zero and one hundred. Glycemic load, a newer term, looks at both the GI and the amount of carbohydrate in a food, giving you a more accurate idea of how a food may affect your blood sugar level. High GI foods spike your blood sugar rapidly, while low GI foods are safe to eat.

High GI: 70 to 100. Foods with a high GI have a tendency to increase blood sugar levels very rapidly. They have to be reduced the most when trying to control weight. Sugar which is absorbed fast needs the body to release large doses of insulin which increases fat storage. Fat storage is reduced with a minimal release of insulin in the body.

Intermediate or medium GI: 55 to 70. Foods with a medium GI have to be included in moderation in order to prevent weight gain and also spikes in blood-sugar levels.

Low GI: Below 55. In order to achieve weight loss and also keep sugar levels within the normal range, it is always advisable to plan meals from this list of foods. Low GI foods make you feel fuller for a longer time and help control your appetite.

SOME FOODS WITH THEIR GIS:

High GI:

- Baked potato, 85
- White bread, 70
- Waffles, 76
- Weetabix, 77
- Watermelon, 72
- Bagel, 72
- Morning coffee, 79
- Doughnut, 76
- Cornflakes, 83
- Instant porridge, 79

Intermediate or medium GI:

- Croissant, 67
- Sweet biscuits, 69
- Honey, 58
- Digestives, 58
- White rice, 58
- Sugar, 65
- Basmati rice, 58
- Popcorn, 55
- Brown rice, 55
- Couscous, 65

Low GI:

- Noodles, 47
- Baked beans, 48
- Wholegrain bread, 50
- Porridge (non-instant), 49
- Lentils, 29
- Cucumber, 15
- Apples, 36
- Kiwi, 52
- Lentil soup, 44
- Soy milk, 30
- Pineapple juice, 46
- Grapefruit juice, 48
- Pasta, 41
- Multigrain bread, 48
- Burger bun, 61
- Kidney beans, 27
- Broccoli,15
- Celery,15
- Bananas, 55
- Milk, 27
- Yoghurt, 44
- Apple juice, 41
- Carrot juice, 45
- Orange juice, 52

GI for some Indian foods:

- Bengal gram daal (chana daal), 16
- Soy beans, 16
- Rajmah (red kidney beans), 27
- Besan (chickpea flour), 39
- Green gram (moong beans), 54

❖ Chickpeas (chole), 33
❖ Barley (jau), 61
❖ Black gram, 61
❖ Horse gram 73
❖ Whole green gram 81
❖ Bajra (millet), 82
❖ Maize , 89
❖ Ragi (or nachni), 98

Diabetes and diet tip 2: Be smart about sweets

Eating for diabetes doesn't mean eliminating sugar, an often misundersood rule. If you have diabetes, you can still enjoy a small serving of your favourite dessert now and then. The key is moderation.

The good news is that cravings do go away and preferences change. As your eating habits become healthier, foods that you used to love may seem too rich or too sweet, and you may find yourself craving healthier options.

HOW TO INCLUDE SWEETS IN A DIABETES-FRIENDLY DIET

1. Give up on one carb. Go for either the bread (or rice or pasta) or dessert. Eating sweets at a meal adds extra carbohydrates. Because of this it is best to cut back on the other carb-containing foods at the same meal.

2. Eat sweets with a meal, rather than as a stand-alone snack. When eaten on their own, sweets and desserts cause your blood sugar to spike. But if you eat them along with other healthy foods as part of your meal, your blood sugar won't rise as rapidly.

3. When you eat dessert, truly savour each bite. There have been too many times when you mindlessly ate your way through a bag of cookies or a huge piece of cake. Make your indulgence count by eating slowly and paying attention to the flavours and textures. You'll enjoy it more, plus you're less likely to overeat.

Diabetes and your diet tip 3: Choose fats wisely

Fats can be either helpful or harmful in your diet. People with diabetes are at higher risk of heart disease, so it is even more important to be smart about fats. Some fats are unhealthy and others have enormous health benefits. But all fats are high in calories, so you should always watch your portion sizes.

Diabetes and diet tip 4: Eat regularly

If you happen to be overweight, you will be glad to note that you can cut down the risk of getting diabetes by half by just reducing your body weight by 7 percent. Research has shown that you do not need to starve yourself or count calories like a maniac to achieve this. All you need to do is follow a regular eating schedule and record what you eat.

❖ **Eat at regularly set times**: Your body is better able to regulate blood sugar levels—and your weight—when you maintain a regular meal schedule. Aim for moderate and consistent portion sizes for each meal or snack.

❖ **Don't skip breakfast**: Eating breakfast every day will help you have energy as well as steady blood sugar levels.

❖ **Eat regular small meals—up to six per day**: People tend to eat larger portions when they are overly hungry, so eating regularly will help you keep your portions in check.

❖ **Keep calorie intake the same**: Regulating the amount of calories you eat on a day-to-day basis has an impact on the regularity of your blood-sugar levels. Try to eat roughly the same amount of calories every day, rather than overeating one day or at one meal, and then skimping on the next.

12

Liver Issues

IN MY PROFESSION, I MORE THAN OFTEN AM PRIVY TO MANY personal details of the lives of my clients, whether I want to or not. There was one couple who came to me at a time when they were going through a huge personal crisis. It has been one of my most difficult cases not because of the nature of the treatment but because of the nature of the patients. The husband was having an extramarital affair and the wife found out. Her method of dealing with it was to try to make sure that he always stayed at home, with her. The wife made it extremely hard for me to treat her husband; in my first meeting, she actually asked me if I could *give him Alzheimer's*, so that you know he's forget about his mistress and stays only with her!

Meet Jitendra and Hema. Jitendra Sharma, a 33-year-old school teacher, whom I met through his cousin who I was treating for hyperinsulinism and polycystic ovaries, first consulted me with a complaint of painful joints especially of the wrists. About six months previously to our meeting, while working out in the gym, he experienced the onset of acute stiffness of the fingers. His elbow, wrist, and knee joints were very painful. His gym instructor asked him to increase his protein intake and managed to sell a box of whey protein to him. A month after he randomly began consuming this, he noted that his stool had become lighter in colour. He experienced excruciating abdominal pain, weight loss, fever, nausea, vomiting, and lethargy. When he went for medical tests and got his liver tested, his medical reports were: SGOT 113 U/L, SGPT 96 U/L, total bilirubin 1.0 mg/dL, and alkaline phosphatase 73 IU/L. **SGOT and SGPT are liver enzymes, bilirubin is a brownish yellow pigment found in bile, produced when the liver breaks down old blood cells.**

His water intake was less than a litre a day because his classroom was air conditioned he never felt thirsty, so he didn't think of drinking water.

I asked Jitendra to increase his water intake to a minimum of 1.5 litres per day. Lemon juice and cinnamon powder was to be added to the water to enhance the taste of the water as well as to cleanse his system. I recommended a diet which provided him with 45 gm of protein that was sufficient for his current medical status. **And after each meal, I asked him to have 2 tsp of a mix which had flax meal, mint powder, fenugreek seeds, sesame seeds, and bay leaves**.

Within 10 days he reported that the joint pain had decreased and so I asked him to continue taking the same mix. After a month I asked him to add thyme and curry leaves to his mix. Two months later, he had increased weight (muscle mass), his appetite had increased, and the abdominal pain had vanished. He repeated his blood tests and was more than happy to report that his SGOT, SGPT, and alkaline phosphatase levels had reduced by 50 percent. His wife, however, had no comment to make. I followed up with him till he eventually he didn't need the mix at all.

Liver problems include a wide range of diseases and conditions. Your liver is an organ about the size of a football that sits just under your rib cage on the right side of your abdomen. Without your liver, you won't be able to digest food and absorb nutrients, get rid of toxic substances from your body, or stay alive.

Problems in the liver might either be inherited or may develop due to a prolonged exposure to viruses and chemicals. These problems may either be temporary, where the disease might go away on its own, or the problem might be long termed in which case there might be serious complications.

What is liver disease?

Liver, or hepatic, disease is any change or disturbance in the liver's functioning, which results in illness. The liver is responsible for vital body functions and should it become diseased or injured, there may be significant damage.

Usually, more than 75 percent or three-quarters of liver tissue needs to be affected before decrease in function occurs.

What are the symptoms of liver disease?

❖ discoloured skin and eyes that appear yellowish
❖ abdominal pain and swelling
❖ itchy skin that doesn't seem to go away
❖ dark urine colour
❖ pale stool colour
❖ bloody or tar-coloured stool
❖ chronic fatigue
❖ nausea
❖ loss of appetite

However, since there are a variety of liver diseases, the symptoms tend to be specific for that illness until late-stage liver disease and liver failure occurs. **If you are suffering from any of these symptoms, go consult your doctor immediately and get your tests done.**

What are the causes of liver disease?

Damage to the liver can be caused due to:
❖ inflammation of cells (such as in hepatitis)
❖ the flow of bile might be blocked (such as in cholestasis)
❖ reduced blood flow to the liver
❖ liver tissue may be damaged or scarred by chemicals and minerals, or infiltrated by abdominal cells

How do you detect liver damage?

Blood tests: An initial step in detecting liver damage is a simple blood test to determine the presence of certain liver enzymes in the blood. Under normal circumstances, these enzymes reside within the cells of the liver. But when the liver is injured, these enzymes are spilled into the blood stream, raising the enzyme levels in the blood and signalling liver damage. Among the most sensitive and widely used of these liver enzymes are the aminotransferases. They include aspartate aminotransferase (AST or SGOT), and alanine aminotransferase (ALT or SGPT).

AST (SGOT) and ALT (SGPT) are sensitive indicators of liver damage from different types of disease. In rare cases, higher-than-normal levels of these liver enzymes may have causes other than liver problems. The interpretation of elevated AST and ALT levels depends upon the whole clinical picture. The precise levels of these enzymes do not correlate well with the extent of liver damage or the prognosis. Thus, the exact levels of AST (SGOT) and ALT (SGPT) cannot be used to determine the degree of liver disease or predict the future. For example, patients with acute viral hepatitis may develop very high AST and ALT levels (sometimes in the thousands of units/litre range). But most patients with acute viral hepatitis A recover fully without residual liver disease.

Test of the liver: Tests of the liver such as the alkaline phosphate or GGTP test indicate if the bile ducts in the liver are obstructed. Though alkaline phosphates are present in various other organs such as the bone and placenta, GGTP is extremely liver specific. The GGTP levels may rise due to diseases of the bile duct such as cirrhosis and selerosing cholangitis, in acute conditions choledocholthiasis (gall stones in the bile ducts). GGTP levels may also rise dramatically in people who consume alcohol regularly.

What are the risk factors for liver disease?

Lifestyle: Some liver diseases are potentially preventable and are associated with lifestyle choices. Alcohol-related liver disease is due to excessive consumption and is the most common preventable cause of liver disease.

Hepatitis B and C: are viral infections that are most often spread through the exchange of bodily fluids (for example, unprotected sexual intercourse, sharing unsterilized drug injecting equipment, using non-sterilized equipment for tattoos or body piercing).

Hereditary liver disease: can be passed genetically from generation to generation. Examples include Wilson's disease (copper metabolism abnormalities) and haemochromatosis (iron overload).

Chemical exposure: may damage the liver by irritating the liver cells resulting in inflammation (hepatitis), reducing bile flow through the liver (cholestasis), and accumulation of triglycerides (steatosis). Chemicals such as anabolic steroids, vinyl chloride, and carbon tetrachloride can cause liver cancers.

Acetaminophen (Tylenol) overdose: is a common cause of liver failure. It is important to review the dosing guidelines for all over-the-counter medications and to ask for guidance from your healthcare professional or pharmacist as to how much may be taken safely.

Medications: may irritate the blood vessels causing them to become narrow, or can lead to the formation blood clots (thrombosis). Birth-control pills may cause hepatic vein thrombosis, especially in smokers.

Can liver disease be prevented?

You'll be glad to know that the **liver is the only organ in the body that can regenerate itself**, but if the damage is extensive it may not be able to meet all of the body's needs. So be kind to it. Prevent liver problems by protecting your liver. For example:

❖ **Drink alcohol in moderation, if at all**: Limit the amount of alcohol you drink to no more than one drink a day for women and no more than two drinks a day for men.

❖ **Avoid risky behaviour:** Get help if you use illicit intravenous drugs. If you choose to have sex, use condoms. If you choose to have tattoos or body piercings, be picky about safety.

❖ **Get vaccinated**: If you're at increased risk of contracting hepatitis or if you've already been infected with any form of the hepatitis virus, talk to your doctor about getting the hepatitis B vaccine. A vaccine is also available for hepatitis A.

- ❖ **Use medications wisely**: Only use prescription and non-prescription drugs when you need them and take only the recommended doses. Don't mix medications and alcohol. Talk to your doctor before mixing herbal supplements or prescription or non-prescription drugs.

- ❖ **Avoid contact with other people's blood and body fluids**: Hepatitis viruses can be spread by accidental needle sticks or improper clean-up of blood or body fluids. It's also possible to become infected by sharing razor blades or toothbrushes.

- ❖ **Watch what gets on your skin**: When using insecticides and other toxic chemicals, cover your skin with gloves, long sleeves, a hat, and a mask.

- ❖ **Eat a healthy diet**: Eat a variety of fruits and vegetables. Limit high-fat foods.

- ❖ **Maintain a healthy weight**: Obesity can cause a condition called non-alcoholic fatty liver disease, which may include fatty liver, hepatitis, and cirrhosis

Before I move on to the important and often neglected issue of a liver-disease diet, I want to talk about this case, which involved the radical son of an extremely orthodox Jain family.

I was already acquainted with 58-year-old Suresh Singhvi, as I was treating his wife for cancer. Theirs was an extremely orthodox house, especially because of Suresh's mother. So strong were her beliefs that she wouldn't even touch honey, figs, or parsley. Her son, on the other hand, was a hardcore non-vegetarian and a regular drinker since he was 20 years old, but none of this ever entered the house.

Suresh developed jaundice after a business trip overseas. In one of my visits to their house, he complained of severe fatigue, abdominal pain, light-coloured stools, dark foul-smelling urine, and itchiness of the skin. He had already gotten the tests done and his bilirubin level was 26 mg/dL, (conjugated bilirubin, 19.3 mg/dL), SGOT (aspartate aminotransferase) 223 IU/L (reference range: 8-58 IU/L), SGPT (alanine aminotransferase) 103 IU/L (reference range: 8-52 IU/L), and alkaline phosphatase 302 IU/L (reference range: 34-124 IU/L). As expected, in his nutritional assessment he specified that he consumed liberal amounts of alcohol and non-vegetarian food while he was abroad. At home, he was a strict vegetarian and would not have more than 60 ml whiskey a week.

I asked him to start having a mix of dried mint powder, cinnamon powder, flax seeds, fennel, turmeric powder, and cumin powder. After two weeks, fenugreek seeds and poppy seeds were added to the mix. Ten days later, mace and dried celery were also added to boost the effect of the initial mix. I also asked him to have lemon water infused with mint leaves. Within a week, he reported that his urine had stopped smelling so foul. Two weeks later, he reported that the urine colour was pale once again and there was no abdominal pain. But he was still feeling tired. Star anise was added to his mix. When he repeated his liver-profile tests after a month of treatment, his bilirubin levels were down to 7, SGOT was at 63, SGPT at 67 and alkaline phosphatase had come down to 97. It took another month of treatment to bring back his levels within the normal scale.

He still takes a maintenance powder to strengthen and cleanse his liver.

What is a liver-disease diet?

A liver-disease diet provides the right amount of calories, nutrients, and liquids for you. A liver-disease diet may help your liver work better and prevent other health problems. The dietary changes you will need to make depend on the type of liver disease and health problems you have. Your dietitian or nutritionist will tell you about the type of diet that is best for you.

How can a liver-disease diet part of my lifestyle?

❖ Changing what you eat and drink may be hard at first. You may need to make these changes part of your daily routine. Following a liver-disease diet may help you feel better.

❖ Make sure that you choose a wide range of items from this diet so that you avoid getting bored of eating the same thing every single day. Make a list of items you are allowed to eat and keep it in your kitchen to remind yourself.

❖ Always carry this list of items that you are allowed on this diet to remind yourself about it when you are not at home.

❖ Any questions that you have should be asked to your doctor, dietitian, or nutritionist regarding what diet plan you should follow. The dietitian or nutritionist will work with you and help you find the right plan. The doctors will also help you in adjusting with your new diet plan.

What food and drinks should be limited or avoided while on a liver-disease diet?

The food that you technically need to avoid or reduce completely depends on the type of liver disease you suffer from and the other health problems you have. Some of the dietary changes that you might need to make are as follows:

❖ **Sodium**: You might just need to decrease the amount of salt in your diet as it causes your body to hold on to liquids. This retention of fluids causes swelling in the body. Your doctor will suggest you to limit or altogether avoid high sodium foods and will naturally give you more information about a low sodium diet. Some high sodium food stuffs are as follows:
  • bacon, sausage, and deli meats
  • canned vegetables and vegetable juice
  • frozen dinners
  • packaged snack foods like potato chips and pretzels
  • soy, barbecue, and teriyaki sauces
  • soups
  • table salt
❖ **Liquids**: If you have any swelling, you will have to reduce your liquid intake. All juices, sodas, water, milk, and any other beverages along with any food items that contain liquids like soup. This also contains food which melts if

it is not cold like gelatin. You should consult with your doctor about the amount of liquid you should consume every day.

❖ **Alcohol:** Alcohol may make your liver disease worse. Avoid alcohol at all cost.

What can be eaten while on a liver-disease diet?

Eat a variety of foods each day to help your liver work as well as possible, and to keep a healthy weight. You may not feel hungry or you may feel full right away after eating. This may make it hard for you to eat enough calories. Eat several small meals throughout the day instead of large meals to make sure you eat enough calories. Ask your dietitian or nutritionist how many calories you need each day.

It is important to eat the right amount of protein when you have liver disease. Your dietitian or nutritionist will tell you how much protein you should have each day.

Many people who suffer from liver disease have problems with, digestion, i.e. using of fat. The fat that is not broken down and used by the body is lost in bowel movements. If you have this health problem, you may need to eat less fat. Your doctor may also suggest that you eat a special type of fat that is absorbed more easily by your body.

Liver disease may cause blood sugar levels to be too high or too low in some people. You may need to make changes in your diet if you have this problem. Eating a fixed amount of carbohydrates at each and every meal will help to keep the blood sugar levels in check.

13

Prostrate Gland Issues

THE PROSTATE GLAND'S MAIN FUNCTION IS TO HELP WITH THE production of semen (the fluid that transports sperm). It produces a thick, white fluid that's liquefied by a special protein known as prostate-specific antigen (PSA). The fluid is mixed with sperm, produced by the testicles, to create semen.

Three main conditions can affect the prostate gland:

❖ prostate enlargement
❖ prostatitis (inflammation of the prostate gland)
❖ cancer of the prostate

PROSTATE ENLARGEMENT

Prostate enlargement is a very common condition associated with ageing. It's estimated that a third of men over 50 years will have symptoms of prostate enlargement. If the prostate becomes enlarged it can place pressure on the urethra. This makes it harder for the bladder to empty.

What are the symptoms of an enlarged liver?

An enlarged prostate can cause symptoms that can affect the normal pattern of urination. For example, it can:
* make it difficult for you to start urinating
* weaken the flow of urine or cause 'stopping and starting'
* cause you to strain to pass urine
* cause you to urinate more frequently, making you get up frequently during the night

PROSTATITIS

A very misunderstood condition, in prostatitis the tissues of the prostate gland get inflamed, i.e. red and swollen. Inflammation sometimes occurs in response to infection, but in most cases of prostatitis, no evidence of infection can be found.

What are the symptoms of prostatitis?

Symptoms of prostatitis include:
* pelvic pain
* testicular pain
* pain while ejaculating
* pain in the perineum (the area between the anus and back of the scrotum), which worsens with sitting

PROSTATE CANCER

Prostate cancer is the most common type of cancer in men. The chances of developing prostate cancer increases as you get older. Most cases occur in men who are 70 years old or over. The outlook for prostate cancer is considered to be extremely positive, even more so after comparison with other cancers. The reason for this is that unlike the other forms of cancer, prostate cancer progresses very slowly. In fact, men can live many years without any symptoms or treatment; rather they die with it, instead of from it.

What are the symptoms of prostate cancer?

The causes of this cancer are unknown, but its symptoms are very often identical to prostate enlargement. The following are the symptoms:

❖ an urge to urinate more often (especially during the night)
❖ need to run to the bathroom
❖ difficulty in start of urination (hesitancy)
❖ straining or taking a very long time to urinate
❖ weak flow
❖ feeling that your bladder hasn't emptied completely

Food and diet

Food and diet always come to the rescue, and they help in keeping a healthy prostate too. The following information should be helpful in dealing with prostrate problems.

❖ Eat foods rich in phyto-ooestrogens like soya beans, tofu, chickpeas, lentils, peas, garlic, and flaxseed.
❖ Lycopenes found in tomatoes have a protective effect against prostate cancer.

- ❖ Zinc found in fish, shellfish, seeds, and eggs.
- ❖ Fibre-rich foods.
- ❖ Fennel is also used to treat prostate problems.

PROSTRATE HEALTHY

- ❖ Make a mix of dried curry leaf powder, mango powder, pomegranate seed powder, fennel, dried basil, dried thyme, mace, and fennel. Eat 1 tsp of this every morning.

- ❖ Infuse 5 peppercorns in 1 litre of water and drink this daily.

14

Thyroid Issues

THYROID. YOU MUST HAVE SEEN WOMEN GAIN A LOT OF weight in a few months. You'll say it's all the sweets. Sometimes it is. Sometimes it's not. Most often, in fact, it is a matter of thyroid malfunction. In this chapter, I'll talk about the importance of thyroid and how to treat it with the proper remedies.

The thyroid is a butterfly-shaped gland located in the front of the neck just below the Adam's apple. This gland acts like a miniature factory and uses iodine from our diets to manufacture thyroid hormones. These thyroid hormones effect growth and help regulate the body's metabolism among the important functions.

The two most important thyroid hormones are **thyroxine** (T4) and **triiodothyronine** (T3), representing 99.9 percent and 0.1 percent of thyroid hormones respectively. The hormone with the most biological power is actually T3. Once released from the thyroid gland into the blood, a large amount of T4 is converted to T3—the active hormone that affects the metabolism of cells in our body.

Thyroid hormone regulation—the chain of command

The thyroid gland itself is regulated by two other glands present in the brain, namely the pituitary and hypothalamus. It is interesting to note that the pituitary itself is regulated by the hypothalamus as well as the thyroid (through a 'feedback' effect of thyroid hormones).

It is a chain reaction wherein the hypothalamus releases the thyrotropin releasing hormone (TRH), which makes the pituitary gland secrete thyroid stimulating hormone (TSH), which subsequently stimulates the thyroid to release the thyroid hormones.

If over activity of any of these three glands occurs, an excessive amount of thyroid hormones can be produced, thereby resulting in hyperthyroidism. Inactivity or lowered functioning of any of the glands will result in a deficiency of thyroid hormones, causing hypothyroidism.

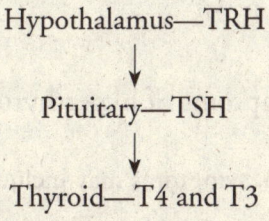

Hypothalamus—TRH

↓

Pituitary—TSH

↓

Thyroid—T4 and T3

The rate of the thyroid hormone production is controlled by the pituitary gland. If there is an insufficient amount of thyroid hormone circulating in the body to allow for normal functioning, the release of TSH is increased by the pituitary in an attempt to stimulate more thyroid hormone production. In contrast, when there is an excessive amount of circulating thyroid hormone, TSH levels fall as the pituitary attempts to decrease the production of thyroid hormone.

There is another hormone that is produced by the thyroid called **calcitonin**. Calcitonin is produced by specific cells in the thyroid gland, and unlike T3 and T4, it is not involved in this regulation of metabolism. Calcitonin is a hormone that contributes to the regulation of calcium and helps to lower calcium levels in the blood. Excess calcium in the blood is referred to as **hypercalcemia**.

What happens if thyroid function is affected?

HYPERTHYROIDISM

It is a condition in which the thyroid gland makes too much thyroid hormone. The condition is often referred to as an 'overactive thyroid'.

What are the symptoms of hyperthyroidism?

In hyperthyroidism, symptoms may include:
* weight loss
* rapid heartbeat

- ❖ tremors
- ❖ excessive sweating
- ❖ heat intolerance
- ❖ anxiety
- ❖ muscle weakness
- ❖ goitre
- ❖ irregular periods

What are the causes and risk factors?

Hyperthyroidism affects up to one in fifty people and can occur at any age, most commonly between 20 and 50 years of age. There are many causes of an overactive thyroid and you may need blood tests and scans to find out what's responsible. The most common reason is when your body's defences falsely recognize your own tissue as an invader and begin to attack it, although we don't know what triggers this attack. This is called autoimmune disease and in this case, it stimulates the thyroid to produce more hormones.

If you have a nodule or growth in the thyroid, it may also produce too much hormone. Rarely, taking certain medicines can make the thyroid produce more hormones. Hypothyroidism is 10 times more common in women than in men and usually occurs over the age of 40. It can lead to high cholesterol levels and increase the risk of heart disease.

Again, there are many causes, but for some it seems to be part of the ageing process. Hypothyroidism is especially common in women after the menopause. Autoimmune disease, both generalized and localized to the thyroid, can make the thyroid less active. Other causes of an under-active thyroid include treatments for overactive thyroid and genetic conditions such as Down's and Turner's syndromes.

Who is likely to develop hyperthyroidism?

❖ **Women are two to ten times more likely than men to develop hyperthyroidism**.
❖ People may need more regular testing if they have had a thyroid problem before, such as:
  • goitre or thyroid surgery
  • a family history of thyroid disease
  • pernicious anaemia, a B-12 deficiency
  • type 1 diabetes
  • primary adrenal insufficiency
  • a hormonal disorder
  • eat large amounts of food containing iodine, such as kelp
  • use iodine-containing medications such as amiodarone, a heart medication
  • are older than age 60
  • recently delivered a baby in the last six months

Getting tested routinely helps uncover thyroid problems.

What happens with pregnancy and hyperthyroidism?

During pregnancy, hyperthyroidism is usually caused by Graves' disease and occurs in about one of every five hundred pregnancies. Uncontrolled hyperthyroidism raises the chance of miscarriage, pre-term delivery, and preeclampsia—a dangerous rise in blood pressure in late pregnancy. Hyperthyroidism in a newborn can result in rapid heart rate, which can lead to heart failure, early closure of the soft spot in the skull, poor weight gain, irritability, and sometimes an enlarged thyroid that can press against the windpipe and interfere with breathing. Women with Graves' disease and their newborns should be closely monitored. Women with hyperthyroidism should discuss their condition with their doctor before becoming pregnant.

What are the symptoms of hyperthyroidism?

Symptoms of hyperthyroidism may be difficult to assess during pregnancy. Some of the symptoms are:

❖ normally, the thyroid gland gets bigger in healthy women when they become pregnant.
❖ that normal enlargement, combined with fatigue, makes a new thyroid problem easy to miss.
❖ a rapid and irregular heartbeat, a slight tremor
❖ unexplained weight loss or failure to have normal pregnancy weight gain are signs that hyperthyroidism could be developing.

Sometimes hypothyroidism turns into hyperthyroidism, and it confuses even the best of doctors. When 36-year-old Raveena first met me, her complaints were frequent nausea, abdominal pain, depression, anxiety, and extreme fatigue to the point of not being able to take care of her children. Her menstrual cycles over the past three months were irregular. She had lost 12 kg in four months, would sweat profusely even if she walked for five minutes, and was always breathless.

A year before meeting me, Raveena had been diagnosed with hypothyroidism. Her TSH levels at that time were between 14 and 19. Her endocrinologist put her on Thyronorm and asked her to repeat her tests after three months. Her levels dropped to 6.4. She missed her appointment with her doctor as she was out of town. Once back, she did not make another appointment as she felt that the treatment was working for her, a mistake that most of us make. She had lost weight, her bowel movement was regular, and she no longer had water retention. She continued with the medication until, all of a sudden, she had a brand new set of problems.

The first thing I asked her to do was to repeat her blood tests. She was shocked when she got her reports. Her TSH was now down to an alarming 0.73! So from hypothyroidism she had now been diagnosed with hyperthyroidism. I recommended a mix of jeera, flax, khus khus, sesame seeds, ginger powder, dried mint, dried thyme, and dhaniya seeds. I also asked her to add 5 strands of saffron and 1 tsp of roasted jeera in her water.

I told her to go back to her endocrinologist with her new TSH levels and he reduced her medication. Two months later when she repeated her tests, her TSH was 1.78. She was no longer feeling anxious, had gained 2 kg, and most importantly her tremors had reduced and her memory had improved! (She had previously spent sleepless nights wondering if she was suffering from Alzheimer's or Parkinson's.)

Three months later her doctor asked her to stop her medication on the condition that she would test her thyroid levels every six months and keep him informed. She still takes her mix and is very happy with her results!

HYPOTHYROIDISM

Hypothyroidism is a disorder that occurs when the thyroid gland does not make enough thyroid hormone to meet the body's needs. Without enough thyroid hormone, many of the body's functions slow down.

What are the causes of hypothyroidism?

Hypothyroidism has several causes including:
* Hashimoto's disease
* thyroiditis, or inflammation of the thyroid
* congenital hypothyroidism, or hypothyroidism that is present at birth
* surgical removal of part or all of the thyroid
* radiation treatment of the thyroid
* some medications

Less commonly, hypothyroidism is caused by too much or too little iodine in the diet or by abnormalities of the pituitary gland.

Hypothyroidism has many symptoms that can vary from person to person. Some common symptoms of hypothyroidism are:

❖ fatigue
❖ weight gain
❖ a puffy face
❖ cold intolerance
❖ joint and muscle pain
❖ constipation
❖ dry skin
❖ dry, thinning hair
❖ decreased sweating
❖ heavy or irregular menstrual periods and impaired fertility
❖ depression
❖ slowed heart rate

However, hypothyroidism develops slowly, so many people don't notice symptoms of the disease.

Hypothyroidism can contribute to high cholesterol, so people with high cholesterol should be tested for hypothyroidism. Rarely, severe, untreated hypothyroidism may lead to myxoedema coma, an extreme form of hypothyroidism in which the body's functions slow to the point that it becomes life threatening. Myxoedema requires immediate medical treatment.

Who is likely to develop hypothyroidism?

It is much more likely that women will develop hypothyroidism as compared to men. Also, it is a lot more common in persons aged more than 60 years. Certain factors can increase the chances of developing thyroid disorders. People may need more regular testing if they:

❖ have had a thyroid problem before, such as a goitre
❖ have had surgery to correct a thyroid problem
❖ have received radiation to the thyroid, neck, or chest
❖ have a family history of thyroid disease
❖ have other autoimmune diseases, including Sjögren's syndrome, characterized by dry eyes and mouth
❖ pernicious anaemia, a Vitamin B-12 deficiency
❖ Type 1 diabetes
❖ rheumatoid arthritis
❖ lupus, a chronic inflammatory condition
❖ turner syndrome, a genetic disorder that affects females over the age of 60
❖ have been pregnant or delivered a baby within the past six months.

Shabnam's first complaint when she met me was that she had put on 20 kg in eight months despite not having made any changes in her dietary pattern! A 29-year-old woman, she also felt listless and complained about fatigue, thinning hair, and tingling in her hands, especially at night. Her periods had become irregular and lighter than before. She was extremely upset about this because she had just married and wanted to conceive as soon as possible. Her voice had also begun to change and she said that she often felt that she was croaking like a frog. Her skin was very dry and she felt extremely cold all the time. Her blood reports confirmed that she had hypothyroidism, her serum thyroid-stimulating hormone (TSH) was 20 U/ml (normal <4.5).

Her dietary recall showed that she was consuming large amounts of crucifers like cabbage, broccoli, and cauliflower. Her evening snack always included a katori of peanuts. She ate mushrooms and tofu occasionally and loved her chocolate-flavoured soy milk. She was advised to immediately exclude all this from her diet. Her detox mix had flax seeds, kadi patta, tej patta, peppercorns, shahi jeera, khus khus, saunf, and kalonji. I also advised her to drink star anise water to boost her energy levels.

At the end of the first month she lost 4.5 kg and was not as tired as before. Her skin was also not as dry as it used to be. She had started walking and was feeling fitter, but she missed her daily fix of peanuts! She had also begun to crave chocolates, so she was asked to take a date, 1 tbsp pumpkin seeds, and 1 tsp of chironji every evening. Within 10 days, she reported that she no longer craved chocolate and peanuts.

After two months, her TSH levels had come down to 12. She visited her gynaecologist who said that she could start planning her family as soon as her TSH value reached 3 U/ml. In the next six months Shabnam regularly consumed her mix, followed dietary instructions, started yoga, and increased her daily workout to an hour. Her hair was now thicker than it had ever been, her menstrual cycle was now a regular 32-day cycle and most importantly, her TSH was down to 3.2 She could be in the same room as her husband and not complain about the fan being switched on, her intolerance to cold had decreased, and there was no tingling in her hands.

I was delighted when she met me last month to seek advice on maintaining her TSH levels and start on a gestational diet!

What should you eat for good thyroid health?

There are some specific nutrients that your thyroid depends on and it's important to include them in your diet.

- ❖ **Iodine:** Your thyroid contains the only cells in your body that absorb iodine, which it uses to make the T3 and T4 hormones. Without sufficient iodine, your thyroid cannot produce adequate hormones to help your body function at its optimal level. Because iodized salt is heavily processed, some recommend avoiding iodized salt and instead getting iodine naturally from sea vegetables (seaweed). **It should be noted, however, that too much iodine can actually trigger thyroid problems and worsen symptoms, so it's important to have a healthy balance.**
- ❖ **Selenium:** This mineral is critical for the proper functioning of your thyroid gland, and is used to produce and regulate the T3 hormone. Selenium can be found in foods such as shrimp, snapper, tuna, cod, halibut, calf's liver, button and shitake mushrooms, and Brazil nuts.
- ❖ **Zinc, iron, and copper:** These metals are needed in trace amounts for a healthy thyroid function. Low levels of zinc have been linked to low levels of TSH, whereas iron deficiency has been linked to decreased thyroid efficiency. Copper is also necessary for the production of thyroid hormones. Foods such as calf's liver, spinach, mushrooms, turnip greens, and Swiss chard can help provide these trace metals in your diet.

❖ **Omega-3 fats**: These essential fats, which are found in fish or fish oil, play an important role in thyroid function, and many help your cells become sensitive to the thyroid hormone.

❖ **Coconut oil**: Coconut oil is made up of mostly medium-chain fatty acids, which may help to increase metabolism and promote weight loss, along with providing other thyroid benefits. This is especially beneficial for those with hypothyroidism.

❖ **Antioxidants and B Vitamins**: The antioxidant Vitamins A, C, and E can help your body neutralize oxidative stress that may damage the thyroid. In addition, B vitamins help to manufacture thyroid hormone and play an important role in healthy thyroid function.

What should you avoid eating for thyroid health?

There are certain foods that should be avoided to protect your thyroid function. These include:

❖ **Aspartame**: There is concern that the artificial sweetener aspartame may trigger Graves' disease and other autoimmune disorders in some people. The chemical may trigger an immune reaction that causes thyroid inflammation and thyroid auto-antibody production.

❖ **Non-fermented soy**: Soy is high in isoflavones, which are goitrogens, or foods that interfere with the function of your thyroid gland. Soy, including soybean oil, soy milk, soy burgers, tofu, and other processed soy foods, may lead to decreased thyroid function. **However, fermented**

soy products, including miso, natto, tempeh, and traditionally brewed soy sauce, are safe to eat, as the fermentation process reduces the goitrogenic activity of the isoflavones.

❖ **Gluten**: Gluten is a potential goitrogen and can also trigger autoimmune responses (including Hashimoto's thyroiditis) in people who are sensitive. Gluten is found in wheat, rye, and barley, along with most processed foods.

Here is a chart with the different foods that are good for the thyroid, along with their nutrition content. There is a wide variety to choose from, so treat your thyroid to a good meal!

Whole foods support your thyroid	
Iodine	• Primary sources: sea vegetables (kelp, dulse, hijiki, nori, arame, wakame, kombu), and seafood (clams, shrimp, haddock, oysters, salmon, sardines), as well as iodized sea salt. • Secondary sources: eggs, asparagus, lima beans, mushrooms, spinach, sesame seeds, summer squash, Swiss chard, garlic
Selenium	Brazil nuts, tuna, organ meats, mushrooms, halibut, beef, soybeans, sunflower seeds (Note: selenium content of land-based foods is contingent on soil substrate selenium levels.)
Zinc	Fresh oysters, sardines, beef, lamb, turkey, soybeans, split peas, wholegrains, sunflower seeds, pecans, Brazil nuts, almonds, walnuts, ginger root, maple syrup

Whole foods support your thyroid	
Copper	Beef, oysters, lobster, shiitake mushrooms, dark chocolate, crabmeat, tomato paste, pearled barley, nuts, beans (soybeans, white beans, chickpeas), sunflower seeds
Iron	Clams, oysters, organ meats, soybeans, pumpkin seeds, white beans, blackstrap molasses, lentils, spinach
Vitamin A (beta-carotene form)	Kale, sweet potatoes, carrots, winter squash/pumpkin, spinach, cantaloupe, broccoli, asparagus, liver, lettuce
Vitamin C	Guava, peppers (chilli, bell, sweet), kiwifruit, citrus, strawberries, broccoli, cauliflower, Brussels sprouts, papaya, parsley, greens (kale, turnip, collard, mustard)
Vitamin E	Wholegrains, almonds, soybeans and other beans, sunflower seeds, peanuts, liver, leafy green vegetables, asparagus
Vitamin B2 (riboflavin)	Brewer's yeast, organ meats, almonds, wheatgerm, wild rice, mushrooms, egg yolks
Vitamin B3 (niacin)	Brewer's yeast, rice bran, wheat bran, peanuts (with skin), liver, poultry, white meat
Vitamin B6 (pyroxidine)	Brewer's yeast, sunflower seeds, wheatgerm, fish (tuna, salmon, trout), liver, beans (soybeans, lentils, lima beans, navy beans, garbanzos, pinto beans), walnuts, brown rice, bananas

PART 3

GROW YOUR OWN KITCHEN GARDEN

AS A CHILD, MY HUSBAND WAS EXTREMELY FOND OF GARDENING, a passion which my kids and I share too. Our garden has mango trees, papaya trees, mulberry shrubs, onion plants, coconut trees, and guava trees, all planted by my husband when he was a kid and now taken care of by my kids. Now we've also planted dill, curry leaves, coriander, mint, tomatoes, chillies, and some gourds. We are fortunate to have the space around our home in a city like Mumbai, but even for those who don't, the pleasure of a kitchen garden, however small it may be, is always the same. Take this chance to maintain your own garden and live a perfectly healthy, pesticide-free life.

A kitchen garden is delightfully easy to maintain, and all your ingredients will always be fresh. It is surprisingly easy to maintain and is a great stress buster.

Called *potagers*, the more common French term, a kitchen garden is easy to run and convenient when you're whipping up a meal and you're out of a herb. Now, most of us live in flats and apartments in cities. A kitchen garden doesn't necessarily have to be on a plot of land, as a matter of fact, there are 'container gardens', 'windowsill gardens', and 'balcony gardens' for most of us living in metropolitan cities and facing the problem of lack of space. A windowsill, an unused corner, the stairs—these can all be turned into verdant little corners lush with fragrant herbs and veges.

Always remember to not bite more than you can chew. Kitchen gardening do takes up a lot of time, so remember to start small and take baby steps.

Where to begin?

- ❖ **Space**: First, mark out the areas in your house that gets sufficient light and has the space to host a few pots and containers. While planning on growing a kitchen garden, one of the most important things to consider is space. **Even though there is not much gardening space in urban India, container planting is a very easy solution to that.**
- ❖ **Plants**: If your apartment is small, grow plants that are small. You don't want a plant that grows up to six feet in your one-room apartment!
- ❖ **Lighting**: Irrespective of garden size proper sunlight is essential. Try to ensure that your garden gets enough light, preferably full or partial sun, to keep the plants healthy.
- ❖ **Seeds or saplings**: You can either plant seeds (which you can get at your local nursery) or saplings. Both will work.
- ❖ **Soil**: Choose the right soil for your indoor garden. Some soils hold on to water while others are more porous. Ask your local nursery to help you out with this–what soil to use, and how much to water your plants.

CONTAINER GARDENING

❖ Use plastic take away containers, old buckets, and wire baskets for hanging smaller plants.
❖ Recycle old mugs and buckets.
❖ Don't throw away your empty cans and bottles. You'll be amazed what you can grow in them.
❖ Don't forget to make drain holes in all the pots.

Note: f you're using small containers, make sure that the plants you grow don't have large roots.

How to select which vegetables to grow?

Consider what type of vegetables to grow in your indoor garden. The two important factors while choosing plants is which plants can thrive indoors and secondly, which you can use. Decide clearly what kind of vegetables to grow and plan your space accordingly.

Choose vegetables and herbs based on your kitchen requirements, your knowledge of growing them, and the resources at your disposal.

Also, remember to grow plants according to season. Planting a variety of vegetables, suitable to the changing climatic conditions, will ensure that there is a regular supply of vegetables throughout the year. So, it won't make sense if you grow a winter crop in the summer and expect it to thrive.

> **GARDENING TIP**
>
> Start small with herbs such as coriander or spring onions. They're easy, they grow fast and the first bloom will give you the encouragement to grow other things.

Easy herbs and vegetables you can grow at home

Chives

Chives are happy-go-lucky plants, you can grow them anywhere for they thrive in window boxes and gardens both. They are best grown in full sunlight, but being hardy plants, they grow well in shade too. They will also grow well in almost any average, well drained soil. Just keep in mind that when growing chives in containers, you need to fertilize them once a month and water the plan whenever the compost begins to dry out.

Coriander

Bury a few coriander seeds into a pot and keep watering it regularly with care. You'll see the first bloom very quickly.

Curry plant

Curry plant makes a very nice house plant provided you can give it plenty of sunlight. This plant will need supplemental light if you can't give it six to eight hours of powerful light a day. If you do place curry plant in a pot, make sure to add some sand to the soil for good drainage and water it sparingly. It prefers soil that drains well, full sun, and warm conditions.

Garlic

The three things that you need for a healthy garlic crop are definitely a good sunny location, loose soil, and good drainage. Even though garlic doesn't require any special handling per se, it can often contract a fungus referred to as white or pink rot in cool and damp climates.

Ginger

Get yourself a ginger root, one that isn't shriveled and soak it in warm water overnight. The next day, fill a pot that has good drainage with potting soil and plant it.

Mint

Mint is easier to grow from a sapling than from seeds. Take a spring of mint (make sure that the cut is below a node) and plant it in a moist but not wet pot. Mint likes shade and consistent moisture so don't expose it to direct sunlight.

Peppers

Pepper plant varieties include sweet bell peppers, chilli peppers, and banana peppers. Pepper plants need conditions similar to tomatoes: six to eight hours of sunshine per day and well draining soil. Also remember that they need to watered at an even rate of one inch of water every week.

Spring onions

This is the easiest to grow. Take an onion that is sprouting just a little and plant it. Water it carefully and soon you'll have fresh spring onions in your house. Harvest spring onions when their green tops are one inch in diametre.

Tomatoes

The tomato remains one of the easiest and most successful vegetable plants to grow. Most tomato varieties only need well-draining soil and six to eight hours of sunshine per day. The soil must be kept consistently well watered. Depending on the mature height of the tomato plant, you may need cages or stakes to provide support for the plants.

Tulsi

Tulsi seed is easy to germinate and grow. It prefers full sunlight, rich soil, and plenty of water. Tulsi does well in pots or window boxes. One thing to keep in mind about tulsi is that it needs a warm, humid environment to grow.

There's no feeling quite like seeing the fruit of your efforts—that first leaf, the first vegetable sprouting. I hope you enjoy the benefits of your garden, and continue to grow much more.

I hope this book has inspired you to take your health in your hands and spread the message of healthy living to all your near and dear ones.

Acknowledgements

THE BLESSED TRINITY AND THE BLESSED VIRGIN MARY FOR bringing me to my true calling and helping me every step of the way.

Priya Tanna, editor, *Vogue*, for introducing Milee to me. Thank you Milee Ashwarya for managing to convince me that what I did on a daily basis would make for interesting reading. Trisha Bora for the immense support and encouragement she offered all through this project including the photo shoot. Lubna Amir for the reference work.

Dr Gaurpriya Koppikar, head of the dietetics department, Bombay Hospital, for being my mentor and guide.

My clients for having implicit faith in me, constantly recommending me to others, and goading me to write a book on health.

My mum, who encouraged us to eat healthy, my dad who was my inspiration for the spice powders.

My husband Savio and daughters Charlyene and Savlyene for their love and unconditional support...and also for relishing the rajma burgers, soya pizzas, fruit smoothies, carob cupcakes, spinach brownies...as well as asking for seconds! I love you guys.

My brother, Chelston, sister, Laraine, and their families, in-laws, aunts, uncles, cousins, nephews, nieces, and friends for being there and encouraging me and also using the spice powders to stay fit and healthy.

Thank you from the bottom of my heart. I am truly blessed to have you all in my life.

A Note on the Author

CHARMAINE D'SOUZA IS A CONSULTANT NUTRITIONIST WITH more than twenty years of experience in assisting clients who are interested in improving their health through better nutrition and natural care. Her vast and diverse network of clients includes celebrities and industrialists, all bound by the common cause of good health, the natural way.